Wed Into War

Written by Tyson Morlet

Copyright © 2020 by Tyson Morlet
All rights reserved. Written permission must be secured from the publisher to use or reproduce any part of this book, except for brief quotations in reviews or articles.

Unless otherwise noted, Scripture quotations are from The ESV Global Study Bible®, ESV® Bible Copyright © 2012 by Crossway.

All hyperlinks to external websites were intended for 2020. Publishers are not held responsible for any that are no longer valid.

Published in the United States by SGM Publishing in Austin, Tx.
Cover Design: Mira Lou and Jules Morlet
Edited by: Lunabea
Layout by: Julia Weaver

www.wedintowar.com

Library of Congress Cataloging-in-Publication Data

Morlet, Tyson.
Wed Into War : how the gospel marriage unravels the curse / Tyson Morlet.
ISBN: 978-1-7355173-0-8 (paperback)
ISBN: 978-1-7355173-1-5 (ebook)
ISBN: 978-1-7355173-2-2 (audiobook)

How the Gospel Marriage Unravels the Curse

For Jules.

May our love be long and our legacy even longer.

Contents

1. Wed Into War 3
2. The Curse 11
3. Unraveling the Curse 37
4. Fighting Fair 55
5. The Gospel Divorce 79
6. Let's Talk About Sex 105
7. Unraveling the Past 123
8. The Fruit 143
9. Legacy 161
10. The Gospel Single 181
11. The Gospel Marriage 193
Appendix 201

Forward

To write a good book on marriage, you have to have a good marriage.

Obvious right?

Tyson and Jules have exactly that. They have learned what all couples must learn if their marriage is not only going to survive, but truly thrive. So, many couples settle, or worse, give up. Tyson and Jules have done the hard work to build something truly special.

Over the last few years God has used them over and over to repair broken relationships and give hope to many whose marriages were literally at the end. In 'Wed Into War' Tyson takes us on a journey. This book is a perfect blend of practical information, rare insight, humorous antidotes, and timeless proven scriptural truth. It's woven together in a way that is easy to read and even easier to apply.

Three groups of people will greatly benefit from 'Wed Into War'. Those who are starting their marriage journey will find wisdom and insight to avoid many relational pitfalls. Those whose marriages are in trouble will find both inspiration and a clear pathway through their current struggles. And those with healthy marriages will find encouragement to make their bonds even stronger and more endearing. My wife, Laura, and I have been personally and richly blessed by Tyson and Jules, and I'm so looking forward to 'Wed Into War' having the same impact on you and your marriage.

Pastor Rob Koke
Lead Pastor of Shoreline Church in Austin, TX

Chapter

Wed Into War

　　I remember sitting on the opposite side of the closed bathroom door from her in our newlywed apartment with tears in my eyes and enough adrenaline running through my veins to lift a car. I could hear her muffled sobs, and I felt so many things at once: anger, sadness, despair, regret, pity. Why was this so hard? Why was this person that I loved so much so angry, and how could that little one hundred and twenty-pound woman have the power to make me want to curl up into a ball and hide in the closet?

　　I read the books. We did the pre-marital counseling, but nothing could have prepared me for the collision course that is marriage: two half-independent twenty-somethings jammed together in four hundred and fifty square feet, navigating childhood trauma eruptions and in-laws. Whose idea was this, anyways?

　　Turns out it was God's.

Way back even before the beginning, He had much more than happiness in mind for us, even more than holiness. But wait, I'm not ready to jump into the cliché marriage-book-Genesis-wedding quite yet; don't worry, we totally will, just not yet.

Wed Into War

This glorious idea of marriage was in the mind of God, before clay-dirt Adam took his first breath, before Adam named the first beast, before Eve was pulled from Adam's side, and even before Eve named her first son. This idea was a mystery hidden in the heart of God, and all of the heavens waited to see what the heck He was up to.

Oh yeah, there were heavens and angels and stuff before the first marriage. They were on the guest list to the first wedding, no doubt filled with wonder at this new thing God was doing. Okay, okay, I'm doing the cliché thing again. Sorry. We'll get there. But what I want to focus on right now happened before Adam and Eve.

WE ARE WED INTO WAR

We are wed into a war between God and His enemy. This is a weird place to start a book on marriage, I'll admit, but hey–this is where it needs to begin. I need you to understand that marriage is very hard before we even buy the diamond.

Look at it this way; the Bible teaches that there was a whole story that happened before our story. There were created beings before us called angels. I'll spare you the details, but there was a coup. There was an angel named Lucifer that tried to take the throne from God. He mostly failed, but he was able to convince one-third of the angels to go with him.

When we think "angel" in the west, we think of a peaceful white man with a harp and amazing hair, but the bible teaches that these beings were valiant warriors. In some instances, a single one of them was able to defeat whole armies of men by themselves! Every time they would try to talk to a person, the first thing they would say is something like, "You're okay, I'm not going to kill you, please chill out, I swear I just want to tell you something!" because these creatures were absolutely terrifying.

If you think your family drama was bad before your wedding, well this was the temperature before the first wedding! It was an absolute war. God violently cast Lucifer and his followers from heaven somewhere between Genesis 1 and Genesis 2[1].

Then, He took a breath, and He made man.

The creation of Adam and his marriage to Eve was a declaration of God's victory to His enemy before the dust of this war had even settled. I imagine that it was a huge slap in the face. Lucifer takes a third of God's created beings, so God goes on and makes new ones! Wow. Audacious, to say the least.

Then He marries them to each other. He establishes a new idea: an unending covenant, a promise, that there will be no more coups, no more betrayals, and that this one is built to last. With this covenant, He gives us gender, babies, and finally, family. All these new and unbreakable mysterious relationships and ideas had to have pissed Lucifer off real good. Have you ever wondered what was up with that whole snake thing in the garden? Wonder no more.

Satan (Lucifer has many names) has been hell-bent against our marriages working out from even before the very beginning.

---

1. It would seem since Jesus references the moment he saw Lucifer cast to the created earth in Luke 10:18

THE FAMILY OF FAMILIES

Your marriage has a big ol' target on it because out of it comes the family. God's people can be defined as a family of families. Satan understands that if he can destroy the marriage, he dismantles the family, and if he can dismantle the family, then he disarms the people of God.

Marriage isn't supposed to be easy; it's a fight. Every day you go to war to shut up the lies of the enemy, love your unlovable spouse (while you yourself are also unlovable, by the way), bring some kids up to be ready to keep up that fight and declare that love wins in the end. It's hard; it's damn near impossible, actually.

If I'm right, then I might have just shown you that marriage is actually way harder than you might have realized before you even opened this book. Or maybe I just put vocabulary to why this has been so hard from the beginning. Perhaps I just opened your eyes to the fact that your marriage is under a constant and strategic assault by a very real and very incensed enemy. He doesn't want it thriving, no way. In fact, he wants to open up a full six-pack of suck all over that thing right after kid number three so you can leave your spouse and send your kids spiraling into the chaos of the broken home, ensuring their risk of repeating the same dang thing is exponentially increased. Wicked plan if you ask me.

After the fall of man, God made a promise to Eve– what a cool way to respond to the most epic fail in all of human history. He said something like "One day, your son will crush my enemy's head, though he will get bitten in the heel."[2] As if marriage doesn't

---

2. Genesis 3:15

have enough stacked against it, God actually reveals his plan to both Adam and Eve, and Satan.

Why in the world would God reveal his battle strategy to his enemy? Well, maybe it was because He needed us to know that in the end love wins. In the end, the marriage is sustained, the family is intact, and through that family of families would come Jesus.

Everyday that we bend God's grace over to our spouse we are declaring this gospel. We are shouting to a hopeless and broken world that there will be no more coups, and that the head of our enemy is being crushed more and more under the weight of the glory of Jesus.

THE GOSPEL MARRIAGE

This book is not just a book on marriage. It's not "seven habits for a healthy blah blah." It's not "how to love your wife with all the love languages in an order that pleases her ever-changing feminine heart." It's a call to arms. It's a wakeup call to the sleeping church: too long have we slumbered and watched marriages break all around us; too long have we stayed silent; too long have we hidden our shame, alone like silos locked in suburban tract homes, pretending it's all good. It's not good. We're in a war, and we're taking losses.

Okay. Enough bad news, here's some good news– we have the tools to win this war.

We have a brave and fearless warrior leader, Jesus, whose victory was promised to that snake before Eve even had her first son. Not only that, but the Bible gives us everything we need to unravel the curse that for millennia has stolen our legacies from us and our children. Oh and this – the gospel, the story of Jesus – restores everything to us that has been lost. It not only promises future victory, but it recovers past losses.

Furthermore, it actually props our marriages up as a sign of victory to our enemy. The gospel marriage is our greatest weapon and prize. It promises us a life of legacy and shameless belonging. It invites us into the great story of Jesus. It writes our marriages and families into the story of the gospel.

SOME EXPECTATIONS

This book is going to be a journey into the mind and heart of God for marriage. We are going to see what the bible has to say about its origin, its failings, and how the gospel returns it to what it was always meant to be. **My chief hope is to make much of Jesus and the calling of marriage that you might be spurred to join me in the fight.**

Second, I'm really hoping **to spark in you a passion for the Bible.** What the Bible has to say about relationships and the complexities of our lives is absolutely profound. It pinpoints the problem with authority and precision, shows our inability to solve that problem on our own, and then hits us in the face with the realization that Jesus, the answer to the problem, was interwoven all along!

When I realized what was at stake so much came into view for me. When I realized what was really lost if I quit, I had an overwhelming sense of responsibility and a fire that burned in me to not only be the best husband and father I could be but also to set free marriages all around me. I now see marriage as this hidden force that brings heaven down to earth one couple at a time!

One of the enemy's greatest lies is that what's at stake is our happiness. My friends, there is so much more to lose. Happiness is as fleeting as sand through your fingers, but the legacy of the gospel marriage is like the ocean's edge – a vast and wild frontier to be discovered.

This book – really no book – can be a stand-alone guide for a good life. Even the Bible is meant to be lived out in community. I believe intrinsically that even marriage is supposed to be done in the context of community. That's why we have a wedding, so people can watch us make the promise and hold us to it. So, grab some friends, go through this book, read a lot of the Bible's thoughts on marriage, and let's walk together.

NOT FOR THE FAINT OF HEART

And now, a warning: what's coming is not for the faint of heart.

I applaud your courage to get this book, open it up, and make it this far. But, what's coming in the following pages will open your eyes to the fight for marriage, calling you to push to fast resolution, to lay yourself down for your spouse, and it will amplify what you know deep in your soul: that your marriage is about so much more than you, or merely this life.

The effects of your marriage reverberate in the eternal. Sorry, not sorry.

Proceed with caution and, more importantly, with wonder.

Chapter

The Curse

The idea we explore in this book was discovered almost by accident one evening. Jules (my wife) and I were counseling a couple who was really going through some hard stuff, and I had this realization that what they were going through was not only outlined in Genesis but was actually *predicted* of every marriage relationship.

In fact, the first problem in marriage, and its consequences, is telling of the reality of the central problem the marriage has experienced all the way through to today's marriages. Not only that, but this truth spoke deep to the core of the issues my wife and I had gone through, dealt with, and are still finding slow steps towards victory in.

It was only once I had this language and could identify the problem easily because of this thirty-five-hundred-year-old document that I started to see couples' eyes light up. Finally, someone had shed light on what they have been trying to put language to for years (ya know, in Genesis, on like page two, but whatever).

Couples started referring other struggling couples to us. We started meeting with so many, digging through so much hurt, years of neglect, seemingly wasted decades, broken kids, and again and again, eyes would light up, and a new hope and excitement would fill the room. It's like we were finally understood, and the darkness that made this covenant so hard to keep was finally explained and exposed.

It's crazy to me that something as simple as identifying a problem, even before a solution is offered, can break through the fog of years of miscommunication. Those counseling meetings turned into a seven-week intensive. By that time I knew, we were on to something.

By the way, it would not hurt to grab a Bible and open up to Genesis 2 right now. You don't have to, as I will give the scripture and references, but it will help your mind grab this narrative if you see it laid out.

Also, it's worth noting that Genesis 1 and 2 repeat themselves but with added details. It's kinda like a Spanish telenovela – you get to watch it go down, then you get to watch em' talk about it!

THE FIRST HUSBAND

"Then the Lord God formed the man of dust from the ground and breathed into his nostrils the breath of life, and the man became a living creature."[1]

---

1. In Genesis 2:7 there's a wordplay we miss in the English. Adam, in the original Hebrew, means *red* like the color of man's skin and blood. *Adamah* means *out of the dirt*. The text literally says, God breathed adamah Adam, or to say God breathed his life into the dust, and it became blood-filled skin. Pretty cool, since blood will be a symbol of life for the rest of the scriptures.

The Curse

Adam was made from the dirt. I don't think we realize the significance of that statement. His terrain is the dirty wild and unknown; it's where he started and it's where he's always trying to get back to. In fact, he's like God in that.

When God was ready to create man he went to the dirt, the chaos, the untamed land, and then he formed it into Adam and breathed into it. He put his life in the dirt and it became life. That's what Adam does. He sees the dirt, he forms something out of it, and then he makes it into something that resembles himself, chaos into order, nothingness into life.

And that's not all. God then gives him a job. A big CEO-sized one, in fact. "Now out of the ground the Lord God had formed every beast of the field and every bird of the heavens and brought them to the man to see what he would call them. And whatever the man called every living creature, that was its name"[2] Name every animal? Think of the scope of this project, the responsibility, the intrinsic danger, and the challenge! A giraffe is a giraffe because Adam was faithful to this project, a toad a toad, a lion a lion.

He didn't shy away from this task. Imagine the danger of tracking these animals, the creativity required to name them, and the work to document and remember each name. The most amazing part of all of this is that God accepts the names Adam picks! It's as if He has welcomed Adam into the massive project of creation!

It would be wise for us to keep this on the forefront of our minds: man was created to journey into the wild frontier, name it, and turn it into order. Man was created from the wilderness, and for

---

2. Genesis 2:19

the wilderness. He is up to the challenge of facing every wild thing. He is equipped, then, to go into the uncharted territory of woman. No matter what, he's got what it takes to explore that ever-changing terrain. He did then, and you do now.

THE FIRST WIFE

Adam names all the animals and quickly realizes there's no one suitable for him. It's interesting to me that with all the work to be done, he still longed for more. You might expect God to make Eve from the dirt as he did with Adam, but he doesn't. He makes her from Adam's side – or his rib or some part of him.

The Hebrew here is ambiguous, but one thing is clear – she is made from him. He is her terrain. He is her great unknown. He is her frontier, and we have been re-telling their story for millennia. The beauty showing the beast how to love. She is the princess waiting for her prince to come!

A GREAT GOD AND A GREAT CALLING

We are created to take in all that is beautiful with awe and wonder! Look how Adam responds when God brings him Eve. He becomes a poet instantly!

"This at last is bone of my bones
and flesh of my flesh;
she shall be called Woman,
because she was taken out of Man."[3]

---

3. Genesis 2:23

The Curse

How beautiful is this picture? Adam names her. This is the first task God had given him before there was even an Eve. He calls her woman, *Isha*, which means out of *Ish*[4]. This is beautiful and profound. In giving Eve the title *Isha* he identifies himself as *Ish*.

It's like he didn't know what he was until Eve was created as a reflection of himself. This is to show they were essentially and at a fundamental level always destined to be bound to one another. In meeting Eve, he has met himself.

The more you know and understand your spouse, the more you understand yourself. This is by design.

Do you think Adam was thinking about the alligator or the chimpanzee in this moment? Heck no! His total attention was on his bride, his wife. The skills that he refined on the wild frontier naming zebras and turtles, he now uses with his bride. He claims her as his greatest prize, the best thing to ever come from him, the best part of him. She is his crown jewel and naming her his greatest accomplishment. Adam was created to feel all these things! Eve was created to be the object of his attention.

Now, you might be asking here, what about God? Isn't God enough? Why does Adam need Eve? This is how great God is – it's in the mutual desire husband for wife and wife for husband that an exponential expression of God's love can be discovered! We worship God when we love our spouse. We were created to walk together after God's heart.

---

4. It's worth noting that Adam will not "name" woman "Eve" until after the fall in Genesis 3:20. I think this is significant to the idea that he doesn't have traditional biblical "headship" over her until after the fall.

God's not even close to done being great. He gives them a wedding present. He blesses them, and then He gives them a job to do together. This job would give their life meaning and eternal value. This would give the marriage a purpose so much bigger than themselves, and that mission would keep the marriage full of vision and wonder! Marriage may have been founded in the garden, but it was designed for the wild and unknown frontier!

"And God blessed them. And God said to them, "Be fruitful and multiply and fill the earth and subdue it, and have dominion over the fish of the sea and over the birds of the heavens and over every living thing that moves on the earth." And God said, "Behold, I have given you every plant yielding seed that is on the face of all the earth, and every tree with seed in its fruit. You shall have them for food. And to every beast of the earth and to every bird of the heavens and to everything that creeps on the earth, everything that has the breath of life, I have given every green plant for food." And it was so."[5]

We can get this out of whack. In fact, I thought for years this was Adam's job, and Eve was supposed to support by taking care of the babies at home. Geez, was I wrong. This is their job *together*!

They were to have mastery over the earth, steward all creation, care for it, bring order to it, and fill it with babies. What an adventure! When did we start thinking this was solely Adam's job? How many couples do I see missing this! How many marriages have lost the sense of adventure of going into the wild and making something beautiful from it?

---

5. Genesis 1:28-30

The Curse

We have gotten into a pretty bad habit of thinking of Eve as merely Adam's helper. We're not entirely to blame – a poor translation of *ezer*[6] in the Hebrew has us misunderstanding her role, and then compile on thousands of years of the subjugation of Eve and her daughters, and we have gotten pretty mixed up.

This word is better translated, "a strength equal to." I have no doubt that this misunderstanding was the enemy's idea. Imagine what we could have accomplished with Eve in her rightful place these past couple of thousand years? I mean, this same word is used to describe God's character and the Spirit of God! And yet, somehow, my western mind has been fooled into subconsciously thinking she is lower, and then I'm led to believe it's my job to go and steward all of creation, alone, half of what I could be (let's be honest, probably less). Well played Satan, but the game's up.

NAKED AND UNASHAMED

Right after Adam's poem about Eve, God drops one of my favorite sentences:

"And the man and his wife were both naked and were not ashamed."[7]

Now, before you go judging, this is not my favorite because there's nakedness – it's my favorite because there's no shame! Guys, this is the original design! Imagine what your marriage would be like if you could stand before your spouse, known and fully known, your blemishes, your mistakes, that thing you've kept hidden for

---

6. Genesis 2:18 - We've often translated this as "helper" in the english.

7. Genesis 2:25

years, the brokenness you've never told anyone about, and be fully loved and fully received.

    Naked and without shame. This was always the plan. This was always the power and strength of marriage. And today, it's almost but utterly completely lost.

    We have been fooled into celebrating our secrecy; we have become known as people of hidden darkness. There's literally an "incognito mode" on your internet browser so you can hide what's lurking deep in your soul from the person designed to bring light and healing to that darkness.

    The concept of naked and without shame seems impossible, lost in the decades of our hidden past. But you know what? We're going to get that back. You can stand before your spouse as declared holy by what Jesus has done. More about that in the next chapter :)

THERE'S ALWAYS A DAMN DRAGON

    Ever wonder why there's always a dragon in all those fairytales? Well, wonder no more! There always has been. Remember that thing we talked about a few thousand words ago? We were wed into a war. Do you find it interesting that you don't have to teach kids not to play with snakes? We are inherently afraid, especially my wife! It's hard wired. We've had a real bad experience.

    Satan doesn't wait five minutes to get up in there and attack the first marriage. Genesis 3, verse 1[8]! I mean, it's literally after the naked and unashamed verse. I can imagine him filled with rage.

---

8. Genesis 3:1, I did this to be funny.

The Curse

All he knows is shame; all he knows is the double-edged sword of comparison. Read this literally or as allegory, I don't care as long as you understand that your relationship has a very real enemy, and he doesn't waste any time coming for what God called good.

All right, let's talk about these trees real quick. First, there are a lot of trees in the garden that God set newborn Adam and Eve in, and most of them yielding fruit for them to eat. But, there are two mentioned by name; the Tree of the Knowledge of Good and Evil and the Tree of Life. We make this more complex than it has to be. Think of it this way: Adam and Eve were given two choices; God and "not-god."

The Tree of the Knowledge of Good and Evil was simply the not-god choice. There had to be a choice; there had to be something that was not-god for us to freely choose God. And there still is that choice before us every single day. Every moment, every conversation, every calendar invite, every new show that pops up on Netflix… God or not-god. What about the Tree of Life, you ask? The Tree of Life is more of an idea that actualizes created beings into their states. See this footnote to nerd out on that idea[9].

So, what does Satan do? He starts a simple conversation about that not-god idea. Be careful – he still does this crap today. All the time. He hates your marriage, and he's damn good at kill-

---

9. Without getting too technical here, because this really isn't part of what I want to communicate with this particular book, pre-Genesis, the angels had a *potential* to also choose God or not-god. That potential had a point where it was *actualized* and they were sealed in their fate. This tree represented that for Adam and Eve. That is why it was actually a great mercy for God to expel Adam and Eve from the garden after the fall, so that they would not be actualized in their fallen state before Jesus could come and redeem them. Pretty cool and pretty bible-nerdy.

ing these things. He's had a lot of practice. He approaches Eve and asks "Did God actually say, 'You shall not eat of any tree in the garden'?"[10] What a rascal. Not even what God said at all, like not even close[11]. This is how he operates. He says sex is bad, so we make it taboo and don't talk about it and get all unhealthy, religious, and weird. Not what God said. He says judging is bad, so we gossip instead of exercising just and wise judgment. He's always skewing what God says and pushing life-sucking religion on everything. "What can you even eat?" he asks, taking a shot at the heart and intentions of God. He's hoping to place a tiny seed of doubt in Eve's mind that God is good. And yeah, he still does this today.

Look at Eve's response, "We may eat of the fruit of the trees in the garden, but God said, You shall not eat of the fruit of the tree that is in the midst of the garden, neither shall you touch it, lest you die."[12] Poor Eve. She feels safe with the snake, and why wouldn't she? This is pre-fall Eden here.

She becomes willing to accept a different version of the truth. God didn't say she couldn't touch it. He said don't eat it.

I can just see Eve here, the seed of doubt taking shape. Satan has baited the hook, and now he needs to set it. Look at what he says, "You will not surely die. For God knows that when you eat of it your eyes will be opened, and you will be like God, knowing good and evil."[13] Bold-faced lie. "You will not surely die."

---

10. Genesis 3:1

11. Genesis 2:17 - "You may surely eat of every tree of the garden, but of the tree of the knowledge of good and evil you shall not eat, for in the day that you eat of it you shall surely die."

12. Genesis 3:2-3

13. Genesis 3:4-5

The Curse

Man, what a bummer that lie is. That lie would germinate and grow into something so evil that it would destroy the legacy of families for generations. That lie would tear creation from God and from each other. It would go on to spark genocides and human trafficking. That lie would steal everything. I mean, I get it. Well played.

Eve wouldn't immediately physically die, she would just be set down an inescapable path, where now everything has to one day die.

THE TRICK OF PASSIVITY

So, she chooses not-god and eats it. She checks it out; it looks good; she buys into the superstition that it will make her better, and she eats it. Then she gives some to Adam – wait, where has Adam been? We get in our heads that Eve went and got Adam, who was probably busy harnessing the power of the sun and taming great white sharks, but no, the text says he was *with her*. The Hebrew here literally means "side by side" or "elbow to elbow." He was right there! Watching this whole thing unfold, totally passive to it all.

And aren't we still today, guys? Passively watching justice slide, hiding in our man-caves instead of embracing conversations that actually might affect change in the trajectories of our families? Choosing comfort over confrontation when there is a snake in the damn house lying and manipulating and slowly chipping away at our view of God's goodness? Guys, we've got to stop that. We were designed to stop that.

We have to step boldly into the wild frontier of the uncomfortable to bring it into God's order. We were created for it and we have what it takes to do it.

But Adam doesn't. He chooses passivity. Who is in charge, anyway? Well… Adam. His responsibility was to tend the garden. Look back at Genesis on this, "The Lord God took the man and put him in the Garden of Eden to work it and keep it."[14] This can actually be better translated as "serve and guard it." His job literally is to protect this very one small particular domain, and he stands idly by while everything is destroyed. And why? Because it seemed easier in the moment. Damn it we have to do better.

NAKED AND ASHAMED

One of the saddest verses in the Bible comes next, "Then the eyes of both were opened, and they knew that they were naked. And they sewed fig leaves together and made themselves loincloths."[15] They are now out of design; they are outside of the original intent, and they are filled with shame. Thus begins the great journey of us trying to hide our shame behind fig leaves.

Fig leaves come in all sizes and styles. Rough and tough-calloused husband, servant-of-all wife, but it's all the same – broken people desperate for something to put in front of their shame. I've been doing this for almost four decades. You have too. We would rather carefully construct a very intricate lie than face the truth of our shame.

---

14. Genesis 2:15

15. Genesis 3:7

The Curse

"And they heard the sound of the Lord God walking in the garden in the cool of the day, and the man and his wife hid themselves from the presence of the Lord God among the trees of the garden. But the Lord God called to the man and said to him, 'Where are you?'"[16]

They hide from each other, and they now feel the need to hide from God.

This is the state of most marriages I've encountered; heck, this has even been the state of my own. So how did we get so far from what was intended? We can't pin this all on the enemy; there is so much darkness, even in our own hearts. Where did it come from, and is there a way back to the light? Look at God's response to Adam and Eve: "Where are you?" He is so kind, so gentle. Even now, he beckons at your heart.

Where are you? Where are you and your spouse? Let those questions linger for a moment. Let them tug at your hearts for a second. Where are you guys at? What is the state of things – honestly? God is full of empathy; He knows what the marriage relationship is up against. He knows the darkness in your hearts; He is not scared, intimidated, or surprised by it. He sees how you got there, and He has already paved the way out. He knows the lies that took root back then; He knows what agreements you made with the enemy. He sees it all. He doesn't come accusing, or in disappointment; He just gently asks, "Where are you?"

---

16. Genesis 3:8-9

THE CURSE

The next section reveals the state of all of hopeless humanity, left in bitterness and separation from God and each other, because their shame has been uncovered. "But the Lord God called to the man and said to him, 'Where are you?' And he said, 'I heard the sound of you in the garden, and I was afraid, because I was naked, and I hid myself.' He said, 'Who told you that you were naked?'"

Adam had walked in the garden many times with God, no shame to hide, no reason to cover. But something had changed, his shame is all he can see, and now he has this new fallen instinct to hide.

A lot of us are still hiding, and a lot of our marriages are in a state of hiding or ignoring. God asks a timely question that we should also let linger, "Who told you that you were naked?"

Who told you that you have to hide?
Who told you that your Father isn't good?
Who told you that He can't be trusted with the most broken parts of your life?
Who told you to hide from your spouse?

It isn't God who wants you to hide – He's already declared naked and unashamed Adam and Eve good – it's the enemy. He wants you hiding; he is constantly reminding you and your spouse of your shame. That's not God doing that; it is your enemy who is hell-bent on your destruction. It's the enemy who would have you dying behind your fig leaf instead of naked before the one who can make you whole.

The Curse

Adam and Eve have different instincts now that the not-god choice has been made. Look at what happens next:

"'Have you eaten of the tree of which I commanded you not to eat?' The man said, 'The woman whom you gave to be with me, she gave me fruit of the tree, and I ate.' Then the Lord God said to the woman, 'What is this that you have done?' The woman said, 'The serpent deceived me, and I ate.'"[17]

Adam's cursed instinct is to pass responsibility to Eve, and Eve follows suit and passes it right down to the snake. It's crazy to realize that in one sentence, Adam cut himself off from both his partner and his God, "the woman who you gave me." This is his chance to live into his design by taking responsibility for the garden, for himself, and his wife and he instead blames her and he blames God. Why did Adam and Eve pass responsibility? The same reason we do – they were afraid of the consequences. Remember that the command was eat this and die. Adam would rather sell out his bride than face the consequences of death.

Remember, also, that their job together was to bring creation under their stewardship, but now they pass the responsibility off to each other, and finally surrender it to the enemy. He's fine with this, by the way. If you won't take responsibility for where things are at, he's more than happy to step in, take control, and watch it all burn.

What unfolds next is, I believe, the fundamental core issue in the marriage relationship. This will be known as "The Curse" throughout the Bible. This isn't to say that God curses man and creation; rather, understand that this is the natural consequence

---

17. Genesis 3:9-13

of choosing not-god. I love how C.S. Lewis put it, "How can you, being separated from God, who in His very nature is life, not but wither and die?"

THE SNAKE

"First to the snake he says:
'Because you have done this,
cursed are you above all livestock
and above all beasts of the field;
on your belly you shall go,
and dust you shall eat
all the days of your life.
I will put enmity between you and the woman,
and between your offspring and her offspring;
he shall bruise your head,
and you shall bruise his heel.'"[18]

Every time you see a snake slithering around like a drunk weirdo, it's a reminder that things are out of design. It's a sign to remind your heart that creation is now part of the fight. Creation, the animals, and the ecosystems of our planet, are now skewed. It's not the way that it was designed to be, and all of creation feels the effects of this curse. Creation and humanity are not at peace. That's why Paul can say to the church at Rome that all of creation groans and awaits the undoing of the curse[19]. The earth has also been in subjugation because of the curse.

God is so compassionate, though, even in the first indictment of the curse, here is the beauty and revelation of the Gospel!

---

18. Genesis 3:14-15

19. Romans 8, more on that later.

It's like the secret to unraveling this curse is hidden within the curse itself! That enmity between Eve and the snake will be handled by the offspring of Eve – that's Jesus and the cross! More on that later.

THE WOMAN

"To the woman he said,
'I will surely multiply your pain in childbearing;
in pain you shall bring forth children.
Your desire shall be contrary to your husband,
but he shall rule over you.'"[20]

As a natural consequence of the curse, having kids is now really hard – or so I've been told. I don't know or understand what happened after the fall at the molecular and biological level, but everything changed. Light affects us differently, food affects us differently, and everything is now in a state of decay.

The pain of childbirth is now central to the narrative of being a woman. The monthly cycle of the woman's body is now a reminder of that pain, a reminder the pain is coming, or possibly even the reminder the pain won't bring forth her own children. It will be all-encompassing; ever-present and all-consuming, and *it's not the way she was originally designed*. It's impossible to know what the original design was, but it doesn't take much to imagine a better way.

This taking the central theme of a woman's early life can tend to put some other things out of balance. The pain is so excruciating and the journey of child bearing so vast, that it can tie

---

20. Genesis 3:16

the soul of that woman to her offspring in a way that was never intended.

Remember, Eve was made from the man's side, and she was designed that he be her great wild frontier to be explored. When was the last time you heard of a woman grabbing her husband and leaving the kids?! That narrative doesn't occur – she grabs the kids and leaves the husband every time. I'm *not saying* she should ever stay in an abusive situation, but I think it's interesting that the struggle to put the husband relationship above the kids is a real struggle, and it goes all the way back to the curse.

The next sentence has been used to subjugate women for centuries: "Your desire shall be contrary to your husband, but he shall rule over you." What an interesting phrase.

Another understanding of the translation seems to say, "Your desire will be for your husband's rule, but he will rule over you." Everywhere we see this phrase in the Bible it's talking about the covering the husband has over the wife.[21]

Ever want your husband to do better, or lead better?
Ever want him to be the one to initiate family prayer, couples devotionals, or date nights?
Ever want him to be around more, or be more present when he is around?
This is the result of the curse. The woman wants to take the lead, and she feels like she has to because of the lack of leadership coming from the man. It's the curse.

---

21. Numbers 5:19, 20, Judges 14:15, Ruth 2:11

When Eve ate the fruit, it changed the way she saw Adam. No longer was he this wild explorer and artisan who brought lions and tigers under his leadership; he was now the one who stood passively by while Satan spun lies like pearls with which she could adorn herself.

His weaknesses became all she could see. And so it goes onto today. She will make passive aggressive statements at first, nipping at him and nagging at him, slowly withering him away. Then she will become more aggressive until, finally, he actually becomes her worst fears, either exploding with aggression, becoming limp and completely checked out, or he walks away completely. It's a self-fulfilling prophecy; it's the curse, and it's all laid out here in Genesis – ya know, like a few millennia before you even said "I Do." It's the core issue for the wife,[22] and it always has been, but you know what? It doesn't have to be.

THE MAN

"And to Adam he said,
'Because you have listened to the voice of your wife
and have eaten of the tree
of which I commanded you,
'You shall not eat of it,'
cursed is the ground because of you;
in pain you shall eat of it all the days of your life;
thorns and thistles it shall bring forth for you;
and you shall eat the plants of the field.

---

22. I feel the need to make a caveat here. I'm talking in the general for most marriages. Some marriages are traumatically affected by abuse, and that becomes, as it should be, the central problem. Abuse is also a result of the curse in my view. We will be talking about the long-term generational curses that develop and germinate into these kinds of nasty situations in chapter 7.

By the sweat of your face
you shall eat bread,
till you return to the ground,
for out of it you were taken;
for you are dust,
and to dust you shall return.'"[23]

It's interesting to me that with the snake and with the woman, God gets right to the consequences of the not-god choice, but with Adam, he clarifies the why. Satan orchestrated this whole thing; Eve was tricked, but Adam knew exactly what he was doing. It's also worth reminding that Adam was given the instruction not to eat of the tree; we don't get to see how and when he informed Eve, but the instruction was explicitly given to him[24].

I think what's going on here is that God is saying, "since you found it so easy to listen to someone else's voice over Mine, the giver of all good things, everything that's worth having will be difficult to attain." This isn't about Eve taking authority over Adam; it's about Adam giving up on God's authority so quickly. And so, Adam will have to work, sweat, bleed, and toil that ground to get fruit to come up. There will be weeds and thorns. What used to be a free gift in the garden would now take a whole lot of time and energy.

You see, that's the problem with the curse for man, is now all his focus is off his wife and the adventure they are called to together, and onto his work. It consumes him. It drives him. It's all he can think about when he's at the office and it's all he can think about when he's at home. And the enemy is happy with this. In fact,

---

23. Genesis 3:17-19

24. Genesis 2:17

he wants it to be so difficult to get ahead that the man has to obsess on it.

It's a clever little trick because man will fool himself into believing that this is how he loves his family – by providing for them. But I've got news for you – they might be in a warm home with full bellies, but they are starving for your attention and affection, and they are starting to question the goodness of God.

The man has been tricked. It's all here in Genesis 3. Look what it says, "you shall eat of it… by the sweat of your face… till you return to the ground, for out of [the ground] you were taken; for you are dust, and to dust you shall return." It will all be meaningless. You will spend all of your energy winning at work, and you will lose the world.

BAG IT, TAG IT

Another result of the curse is that man's drive is now often misplaced. We see this when he first woos his wife. He has no problem going to work to get it done, and then putting all his focus and energy on getting the girl.

He will spend sleepless nights joyfully designing flower arrangements and planning elaborate trips up the Pacific coast, all to win the girl. But, once he's got her, he bags it, tags it, and his passions move to the next challenge. This is because the curse convinces man to work for the fruit, and once the fruit is attained, to move on to the next plot of ground.

The problem with this thinking is that the woman is not created from the ground! She is created from man's side and designed to be his partner in the mission of subduing the earth and bringing fruit from it. The design was always for woman to be a strength equal to man; perfectly fit to help him bring fruit from the ground.

SET UP TO FAIL

"Then the Lord God said, 'Behold, the man has become like one of us in knowing good and evil. Now, lest he reach out his hand and take also of the tree of life and eat, and live forever–' therefore the Lord God sent him out from the garden of Eden to work the ground from which he was taken. He drove out the man, and at the east of the garden of Eden."[25]

The next part of the curse is easy to miss; the consequences are almost immediate, and the effects still reverberate today. God kicks them out of the garden.[26] They are made to be homeless. Ever wonder why wives long for security? It's been that way since Eve. Ever wonder why husbands will hustle to provide for the family that grows ever more distant from them? It's been that way since Adam. Ever question the goodness of God in His provision for you? It's been that way since Eden.

---

25. Genesis 3:22-24

26. This is hard for us to see, but this is all an act of grace by God. Again, if Adam were to eat the tree of life he would be actualized in his sinful state forever and there would be no redemption for him. It wasn't about punishment, it was about setting us up for the story of Jesus. It's also worth noting that Adam needed to leave the garden where things grew, so that he could live out the curse where things didn't grow. This is so true of all of life. Where God is, things grow. The burden of the curse is to go where things refuse to grow and bring growth. It's an uphill battle that we just can't win; we do a damn close job, though. It's like that carrot at the end of the stick; the faster we run, the more out of reach it becomes.

The Curse

Back in the original design, "The Lord God took the man and put him in the garden of Eden to work it and keep it."[27] This is the job description of Adam, and now with him, Eve. This can be understood that we were to serve it, protect it, and guard it. There is an irony here because by the end of the next chapter God will have to set an angel to guard it from us, and so it goes on to today – we are destroying the planet as we destroy each other.

The marriage covenant has a lot going against it. There is a very real enemy who is hell-bent on its destruction, there's a new instinct that pushes us to choose not-god, and now there's a curse that sets us spinning into a system that has us set up to fail.

The woman is focused on her babies and "fixing" her husband, and the man is focused on work and providing for his family in a structure that will steal it all anyway. We watch this work itself out every day. The man comes home from a long frustrating day to crazy kids and a half clean house, ready to explode on a woman who's mad that he's home late again because she needs help with the insanity of kids. Or they both work, and his job always seems more important, or she's overcome with guilt because all she can think about is abandoning her kids; or he gets all his affirmation at work and none at home; or she's finding love finally from someone other than him, or this or that and onto infinitum because we are set up to fail.

---

27. Genesis 2:15

The distance between husband and wife slowly becomes so vast that it is a chasm too wide even to imagine crossing, needing years of expensive counseling, which means they just both have to work harder to make it all work.

Is this striking a chord yet?

We are set up to fail.

The Curse

Chapter

Unraveling the Curse

Are you still with me? That last chapter was tough. We have been set up to fail, with enemies from all sides – even from within! But are you ready for some really good news? The gospel marriage has the power to *unravel the curse*! That's why, right smack in the middle of the curse, God drops that Jesus-sized bomb! Satan would see Jesus on a cross, bruising his heel, but Jesus would crush his head. The cross deals Satan the definitive mortal wound; he's a dead snake slitherin', and now we can take our marriages back.

Here's where it gets really good. What Jesus accomplished at the cross and resurrection began the unraveling of the curse's grip on man. It is the beginning of setting right everything that was broken that fateful day we chose **not-god**. In fact, the Bible calls Jesus "the second Adam,"[1] as in the Adam that's going to look the enemy right in the face, choose God, and then die to accomplish the death that the curse promised to the first Adam. *He's the Adam that gets it right and then offers that victory to us.* He also bears the

---

1. 1 Corinthians 15:45-49 or "last Adam"

consequences of the fall so that the sons and daughters of the first Adam no longer have to. The bible says that He literally "became the curse for us... by hanging on a tree."[2]

So, how do we live into the victory of this gospel marriage? I'm so glad you asked.

A MIRROR OF THE CURSE

Tucked in Paul's letter to the church at Ephesus, there's a section on Wives and Husbands. For years, I thought that it was merely about gender roles and how married men and women should behave,[3] but recently, it blew my mind when I accidentally compared it to the curse in Genesis 3.

It not only offers a stark reflection of the curse with an uncanny resemblance, but it offers the key to unraveling it. Hidden within Ephesians 5 is the Gospel Marriage.

WIVES

Like the curse, the woman is referenced first.

"Wives, submit to your own husbands, as to the Lord. For the husband is the head of the wife even as Christ is the head of the church, his body, and is himself its Savior. Now as the church sub-

---

2. Galatians 3:13 quoting Deuteronomy 21:23, Yeah, this was like planned that far in advance :)

3. The same text is repeated in Colossians 3 and actually has the title added "Rules for Christian Households." What a bummer – this could not be further from the truth.

mits to Christ, so also wives should submit in everything to their husbands."[4]

Okay, wait – before you get all mad at me like, "I thought you were saying women needed to be restored to where they were pre-fall, and then you immediately come out the gate with 'wives submit'?! What the heck man?" You're absolutely right – **this verse has been used to do a lot of damage,** so let's back up to the verse before this passage.

In the previous verse, Paul writes, "*Submitting to one another out of reverence for Christ.*"[5] So here is the picture – **we are in constant mutual submission, constantly seeing who can go lower, and who can serve more**. That's the prequel for "wives, submit." In fact, go ahead and read the full context (as you always should). Paul is painting a picture of how the Jesus' followers should live with one another. It's like the Spirit of God has so saturated your heart and mind that His presence in your life is as obvious as if you were to get totally drunk![6] We are so filled with God that He's flowing out of us everywhere in song, encouragements, and melodies.

I can see how this might sound strange, so let me put it this way: run hard after God's presence. Be where He is always, go where He's going, ask for what He's wanting. Get to point where you are overflowing with God and He has to spill out, and out of this you will naturally submit to one another.

---

4. Ephesians 5:22-24

5. Ephesians 5:21

6. I'm not kidding, check out Ephesians 5:18, which we believed to be a rule but it's actually a metaphor! Cheers!

We messed this particular passage up pretty bad when we put the heading over verse 22, separating it from verse 21. Here's what's crazy about these two verses: in the original Greek, they are actually one sentence. Verse 22 doesn't even have the word "submit" in it, but borrows it passively from verse 21. *Oops.* They read something more like this: "Be submitting yourselves to one another in reverence of Christ, wives to your own husbands as to the Lord."[7] This verse was never even meant to be singled out as a directive to women specifically. *Oops again.*

So, within the context of mutual submission, the woman is called to *go first*. Why? Because this is how she unravels the curse! Remember what the curse said, "she shall desire the role of her husband but he will rule over her." How can man rule over her if she readily lowers herself?

I understand this isn't exactly a popular idea, still, even in this day and age. But, just ask yourself this question right now – *if there is an enemy that is dead-set against your marriage thriving, what kind of spirit does he want you to have, and how would he propagate that mindset into our world?* It's not one of submission; it's not one that declares, "I will go low first." We know how he responds when he disagrees; he rallies those who might be like-minded, manipulates a group, and attempts a coup. And that's exactly how our marriages come under his spell when we rally those we can get to agree with us, and we leave.

The enemy is fine with this outcome. He's pushing for it. Submission is the outcome he can't expect; it's the knock-out punch

---

7. I understand that this verse is also referenced in Colossians 3:18. I chose to unpack Ephesians 5 because it was likely written first and quoted in Colossians and because it goes into much more detail. I believe the sentiment to be the same in both places.

he doesn't see coming. You can be the changing variable in a marriage with everything going against it. It's like Jesus, who defeated his enemy by surrendering to death on a cross. You can't outsmart that, because it's logic that transcends our way of thinking.

There are probably some of you who are thinking, *"Hey, buddy, you don't know my husband. There is no way I can submit to that man!"* This has nothing to do with him – nothing! Look what Paul said, "out of reverence for Christ.... as to the Lord." This is the beauty and wonder of the gospel marriage! You respect as if it's Jesus you're respecting and you actually become like Jesus, since He declares His bride right and holy before God the Father. In fact, verse 21 can be taken to mean literally, "in the manner of the reverence for Christ." **How He reveres, you can now revere; how He honors, you can now honor**. You have Him living in you!

In case you're not convinced, Paul goes on to say, "The husband is head of the wife even as Christ is head of the church, his body, and is Himself its Savior." You see what he's doing here? He's saying, "Look, your imperfect and un-respectable husband is part of the church and therefore under Jesus, and Jesus loves his church and is not done saving all of it, your husband included!" He's not done with your husband yet! He sees what's coming and He's asking you to trust Him... so trust Him, He's not finished yet!

Paul goes on to write, "Now as the church submits to Christ, so also wives should submit in everything to their husbands." This is tough stuff. I'm not expecting this to be all butterflies and sunshine all the time. As an imperfect husband myself, I get it – we are hard to follow. But I can promise you this – there is a great example in Jesus; how he loves the church and how she responds to his leadership is a perfect picture. And you know His gentle touch; You know His patient demeanor with you, and how you respond to it. Bend those same affections towards your husband.

JUST LET GO

It's time to let go. It's time to trust that you can release your control on things and trust that God isn't done yet. I'm not saying the man is respectable, but I can promise he will be. I can promise that **Jesus started something in him,** and **He will work it out** until it's done. I can promise that He's got you. He sees you. He knows what you need.

The curse says, take charge and be the leader; Jesus asks you to trust Him and let go. You are not responsible for your husband's holiness. You are not responsible for what kind of father he is. God is not going to hold you to how much porn he looked at[8] or how much of the bible he has memorized. What the gospel asks of you is, surrender.

HUSBANDS

"Husbands, love your wives, as Christ loved the church and gave himself up for her, that he might sanctify her, having cleansed her by the washing of water with the word, so that he might present the church to himself in splendor, without spot or wrinkle or any such thing, that she might be holy and without blemish. In the same way husbands should love their wives as their own bodies. He who loves his wife loves himself. For no one ever

---

8. Yea we going there, see chapter 6

hated his own flesh, but nourishes and cherishes it, just as Christ does the church, because we are members of his body."[9]

You might notice right away like I did, that the man has a bit more on his plate than the woman, and yet we seem to have "wives, submit" committed to memory far more than the gospel calling for the man.

We should make every effort to make this an instinct because this is absolutely profound. Remember what the curse said to Adam, *"Your mind will be on work, go toil the ground and get that fruit out"*? Look what the gospel says, *"Love. Your. Wife."* It says get your mind off of work and put your focus, your time, your energy, your devotion, and your affections on your wife!

This is radical upside-down thinking. This is the unraveling of the curse! Paul goes on to define this kind of radical love, "as Christ loved the church." Your example is the Warrior Savior, Jesus – you know, the One who stopped the stoning of the woman caught in adultery, the Second Adam who resisted the enemy in His moment of greatest physical weakness, the One who made a group of soldiers fall back just by the sheer gravitas of His presence. This is who you can be like! **This is what the gospel offers you. Put your all into your wife, and see what fruit will come.**

Jesus gave His own life for the church. It's interesting to me that Adam was willing to give up his bride rather than face the consequences of his own sins, but the Second Adam freely gives His life for the sins of His bride. And He didn't just give up his life finally on the cross. Everyday here on Earth was given for his bride. Every step was to walk towards her; every decision was execut-

---

9. Ephesians 5:25-30

ed with her in mind, every moment was capitalized to save her. He took no other wife; He didn't even have a place to live, or more than one shirt, that He might stay true to loving His bride. The Bible also teaches that He currently – like literally right now – is advocating for His Bride's pardon.[10] How different is the Second Adam from the first? He doesn't care what the consequences may bring – He will stand up for His bride.

"That He might sanctify her, having washed her by the washing of water with word."

Remember how I said wives are not responsible for their husbands' holiness? Well, guess what, gentlemen? *You* are responsible for *hers*! God will actually hold you accountable for where your wife is with Him. This is terrifying. This means you are responsible for the spiritual temperature of your home – you set the pace. Your relationship with Jesus is like a doorway for your family to walk through. And believe it or not, they have been designed to wait for your lead in this. This means you need to know the Bible! How can you present her washed by it unless you yourself have experienced its soul-cleansing power? I have found this to be so true.

Jules and I have walked through some pretty tough stuff. During a really intense time in our marriage, we happened to take a trip out to Lake Tahoe. The weather was just perfect, not a cloud in the sky. It was one of those kinds of days where the lake just looked like glass, with the greenness of the trees and the majesty of the mountains reflecting from it. It was one of those kinds of days where you almost couldn't tell the lake from the sky. So, we decided to take the car and hunt for a spot to swim and lay out.

---

10. Hebrews 9:24

It was so beautiful and fitting juxtaposed with the chaos of our very fragile marriage. We were fighting all the time. I felt an intense pressure to be the kind of leader that I just wasn't, and she was feeling unheard, unloved, and unseen. She felt like I wasn't trying at all, when I knew all I was doing was trying to please her.

As we drove and spoke about how this lake looked like heaven on Earth, Jules began to sob. Naturally, I assumed that I had done something wrong. Finally, Jules began to share that she had been fighting for me to become something for so long, that she had forgotten Jesus was also working on me the whole time, and that even though she couldn't see it right then, she knew that Jesus would complete the work. She released me that day. She actually said the words, "*I release you.*"

This changed everything.

I didn't have a fallback plan anymore. I didn't have the woman pushing me along. She stopped begging me to grow up and lead. So, I grew up. I started to wake early to read and talk to God. I needed His vision; I needed His Word; I needed Him. When I understood the calling of the gospel marriage, I realized I needed a vision for my marriage. Then I realized I needed one for my whole family.

All of a sudden, I began waking up before work to seek God and write out where my family was going, who we were, and who I wanted us to be. Her freeing me, her saying, "I accept you as you are, *because of who I know you're becoming"* was what needed to happen to make me want to become the person she was always pushing me to be!

That's the beauty of the gospel; it declares you holy, so you want to become holy.

YOU HAVE WHAT IT TAKES

This is simply a *shift*. Guys, you know how to get something you want. You know the kind of dedication and laser focus that is required to make it at work and in sports, your hobbies, and so on. I've watched men pour twenty hours a week into fantasy football and then complain that their wife is mad about how tired they are when they get home from work.

You've got the passion, and you've got the time. Redirect it. Point it at Jesus. Point it at your bride and watch what God will do. Watch your whole life explode with everything you've ever wanted.

Paul understands men. He says to love your wife like you love yourself. The man spends lots of time taking care of himself. (All the women just said *"Amen!"*) Sometimes, he guards his hobbies like it defines him. Sometimes, he spends hours in the gym, targeting each sub-muscle group individually. Sometimes, he just goes hard on Netflix and envelopes himself into someone else's great adventure.

You know what to do – it's time to redirect all that energy. When you do...Ahh, when you do, dreams for what your family could be will fill your heart! Passions that you thought long-dead will awake, reigniting you with the joy you had when you were first pursuing your wife. You will get a vision for where you are going and how to get there, because where you put your focus is where you win. That's how you were designed.

You might be asking here, "*Hey, man, this all sounds good, but I've got mouths to feed. I need this job.*" Do you, though? Do you need it more than your family? Do you need it more than your wife? Because that's the decision you make every day you go out and get that hustle, and then come home too tired with nothing left to give. No one regrets not working more. No one looks back at a life well-lived and asks why they didn't give more time to their careers.

The regret of the best of men is the time they *didn't* give to their families. The greatest lie of the curse is that it's worth it to work harder because it fools you into believing that this is how you love your family. **They don't need your money – they need your time; they need you.** Present you. Vision-creating you. The you that you were designed to be. The husband and father who dreams up ways to wake the wonder in their wives and kids. The husband who shows how Jesus loves, and the father who shows how God the Father loves. You've got what it takes.

A NEW ME, A NEW YOU

Husbands. Wives. Here's what's crazy about the gospel marriage. When you live this out, you actually get what you have always wanted! It's not like the curse promising that you go through all this striving, all this working, all this frustration, and still have everything stolen from you. You actually get what you always wanted.

Wives, when you let go, the man steps up and becomes the leader you always wanted him to be. Men, when you start loving this radical Jesus-style love, your girl will get tender and want to follow you and a mission will ignite in your heart like fire. It's absolutely radical. The gospel marriage unravels the curse and unites you to your spouse. And guess what? You have what it takes to step into this adventure. You have the Spirit of God and the example of Jesus to walk into. You've been made brand new. You can do this, and, my friends, and it's so very worth it.

Adam and Eve had a purpose together: *subdue the earth, and bring the chaos into order.* It's important that you find something you can put your hands to together.

When you put the gospel marriage to work, you will find that it becomes a launching pad for whatever your heart desires. That's another way you ultimately get what you were always after. The man takes his mind off of work and puts it on his wife, and that blossoms into the most beautiful life-giving purpose! The wife watches the man become shaped by Jesus, and she will follow him into any adventure! It might be a small group you lead together, or a new business, or a new ministry…whatever it is, you become an unstoppable power-couple when you live into the power of the gospel marriage.

THE STAKES ARE ETERNAL

I'm not even to the good part yet.

Look at the next couple of verses:

"'Therefore a man shall leave his father and mother and hold fast to his wife, and the two shall become one flesh.'" This mystery is profound, and I am saying that it refers to *Christ and the church*."[11]

---

11. Ephesians 5:31-32 emphasis added

A mystery in the Bible is not like mysteries we are accustomed to. A mystery in the Bible is something that has been hidden in the mind of God and then in a moment, like a Beyoncé album, is dropped into our time-space all of a sudden, with little to no marketing.

Marriage is not about your happiness. It's not about your holiness. It's not even about you at all! IT'S ABOUT CHRIST AND THE CHURCH. God dreamed this monogamous amalgamation from before our time began so that He could tell a greater story: that Jesus would come, and die, and reconcile a sinful people back to Himself by perfect love, become one with them, and restore creation back to its pre-fall reality!

Every day that your marriage "makes it," every day that you stay, every day that you bend the grace of God out to your spouse, you are a megaphone to a dying world that Life Himself has stepped in and called forth for the lost to return home! And every day you feel like giving up, remind yourself what's at stake.

Right now, the divorce rate in the church is greater than forty percent… IN THE CHURCH! The place that is supposed to be a hub of God's unmerited love and grace is the place where marriage isn't working. We have to turn this around. **We have to show this hurting world that love will win in the end.** What's at stake is too great to give up on because it's hard, or we've fallen out of love, or whatever excuse is in the back of your mind right now.

When I realized the stakes were eternal, it sparked a new passion for me to keep going. When I shared this with my wife, her eyes lit up, and yours can too, because you know in your heart, your marriage is about so much more than you. You know in your soul, that it's about so much more than kids, mortgages, retirement plans, and soccer practice. You know it's like a lamp lit in the darkness, promising a safe place. You know it was meant for greatness. You know it was meant to tell a far greater story – that is, frankly, why you might have found it lacking. This is the story it was meant to tell all along. This is the moment for which it was designed: to show a world that desperately needs Jesus how He loves by bending that same divine love out in and through the marriage.

THE GREATEST ADVENTURE

"'Therefore a man shall leave his father and mother and hold fast to his wife, and the two shall become one flesh'" in Ephesians 5 is actually quoting directly from the creation account in Genesis. Of course, Paul would connect us to the Genesis account because he wants us to make this connection.

The man is called to leave his father and mother, and cleave to his wife, and become one with her. This is a profound reality, and the greatest adventure man can achieve in this life. The word in the Hebrew is *"ehad,"* and it is the same word used to explain "God is one" in Deuteronomy 6. The oneness that can be achieved in marriage is but a type or picture of both the oneness of the triune God and the oneness of Christ and the church! That oneness is achieved through the gospel marriage.

Remember how Adam and Eve were naked and yet without shame before the fall? They were perfectly one: same heart, same drive, same vision, same job, and the same God. The gospel marriage renews that. There is no room for shame when the other person looks at you and fights to look past who you are and unto who you are becoming. The gospel says that Jesus substitutes all your sin and shame for all the righteousness that He is.

The gospel marriage says that when I look at my spouse, I see who Jesus says they are! I receive God's grace and bend it out to my spouse. I love that language, "bend it out" because it is a difficult and physical endeavor at times! Jesus has declared your spouse holy. Who are you to disagree, or even speak negatively to that? Paul writes in his letter to the Romans that, "Those whom he predestined he also called, and those whom he called he also justified, and those whom he justified he also glorified."[12] We are not only justified (a fancy word meaning simply, "just as if I'd never sinned"), but we are glorified in His sight. He sees it as already done.

The opposite of shame isn't pride or approval; **it's actually acceptance**. You unravel the shame of the curse when you look it dead in the eye and commit to being an agent of change. Remember, the enemy has been spinning the effects of the curse and the generational sins over your spouse's family for years, and through you the gospel might be the changing variable that he couldn't see coming. You might be the thing that changes the trajectory of a bloodline, no matter how many generations have been lost.

The power of acceptance, coupled with the power of the gospel to change people, is how God is rescuing humanity.

This is the great adventure. You not only get to watch God do all this and more through your spouse, but you actually get to play a central role in bringing it to pass! Watching my wife grow

---

12. Romans 8:30

into the Christ-like beautiful person she has become, and winning her affections all along has been the greatest adventure of my life.

    We are designed to quest into the great unknown hearts of our spouse and win them again and again, all the while declaring with our love for one another that Jesus is who He said He was and that He is faithful.

Unraveling the Curse

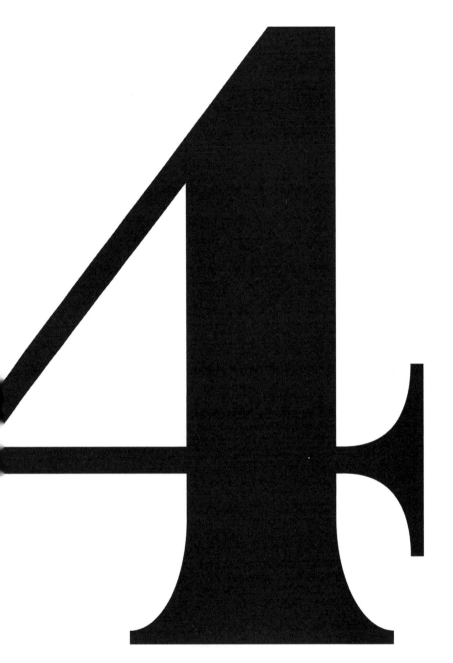

Chapter

Fighting Fair

This idea of the Gospel Marriage is revolutionary and upside-down thinking. If you're like me then your brain is probably spinning a bit right now. Now you know your marriage has an enemy. You've probably picked up on some of his tactics, too. Now you know you're in a war. You know lines have been drawn, shots have been fired, and rescue has been initiated.

You're probably starting to feel a great sense of responsibility to protect what's yours and stop the enemy from taking any more ground in your marriage and in your own heart. You might even be thinking of the places where you're out of balance and need to readjust, reassess, and re-strategize. And I'm sure you understand by now that the gospel marriage is going to take some fight and that some of that fight will be with your spouse!

When I was in high school, I played varsity tennis for about three years. We would practice every day after school, getting our strokes and serves down to a science by doing them over and over. We'd spend hours volleying back and forth in order to form the muscle memory, ensuring that when we needed the perfect backhand or forehand, it was there for us. If you want to win at tennis, then you have to do the work with your team to perfect every part of the game.

When we would practice, our intention wasn't to destroy our partner or even to win – it was always to get better and help them get better. If I approached a practice intending to crush my teammate, then neither of us would get better. If I approached a scrimmage with the idea of making my team better, then it changed the way I played the game at a fundamental level, and we all got better.

This is the kind of mindset we need to develop when it comes to conflict with our spouse. If we approach conflict understanding that its purpose is to, like iron sharpening iron, form us and make us better, then *how much differently would we conflict?*

When we go into conflict wanting to win or hurt our partner because we've been hurt, it actually takes from our marriage and no one gets better. When we rush the net and slam an argument down on our partner, we may win the conflict but lose our spouse, and neither of us can grow. The goal of every conflict with our spouse needs to be strengthening our marriage to withstand our very real enemy and convey the beauty, acceptance, and sanctifying power of the gospel. We need to know how to fight because we have a real enemy. Every conflict you get into with your spouse is a spar so you can develop the fight to defeat your real enemy.

It is a great lie that people cannot change. That is literally a central theme of the gospel; it changes us. God puts a new heart and new instincts in us, but, just like learning our first instincts, these are sharpened and developed on the threshing floor of conflict.

What if conflict in relationships is how the gospel actually changes us?

What if God in His infinite wisdom has given us our spouse uniquely for the purpose of slowly but surely changing us into the image of His Son through the grinding and scraping of our personalities alongside each other?

What if this is the reason why He has chosen the marriage relationship to show Christ and the church?

SET FREE TO SET FREE

Jesus set you free, and you are free, indeed. Everything we do must be a reminder to our spouse of that reality about them. We need to be strategic about the way we fight and the way we take issue with our partner.

The Bible teaches not to let the sun go down on your anger. When we first got married, we would literally stay up till three AM fighting to honor that verse. We noticed quickly that this was setting us up for more failure, more exhaustion, and, therefore, more conflict! Was the Bible wrong? No of course not. My understanding of it was. What Paul is saying here is that time and unresolved anger lead to bitterness. Bitterness, James says, is like a root that will germinate and grow into a huge tree if left unchecked. It's better to push to a quick resolution and dig out that bitterness while it's just a little root.

Anger is a prison, and it's one the enemy will keep you in as long as you are breathing. It's not only a prison for us, but we can also use it to imprison our spouse. You have been set free, so walk in that freedom and declare it over your spouse.

In reading some of the context of what Paul said about anger, a lot more comes to the surface about our conflicts, "Therefore, having put away falsehood, let each one of you speak the truth with his neighbor, for we are members one of another. Be angry and do not sin; do not let the sun go down on your anger, and give no opportunity to the devil."[1] When we lie in marriage, then we lie to ourselves because falsehood enters into the oneness that God has made through us. I love that Paul connects speaking the truth with anger here. That's because it is absolutely okay to be angry. Read it again. Anger is one of the truest and most passionate of emotions.

How freeing is that reality? Get mad. Get pissed. Some issues need to feel the righteous heat of our anger. That's why God gave us that emotion, and you know what? He feels it, too.

I think of Jesus in the temple. He made a whip, turned over tables, and yelled and screamed. His house had been turned into a marketplace of corruption and religious manipulation, and that pissed Him off, as it should. There are things in your marriage and in your household that should piss you off. The enemy has woven in so much hurt and shame, and you have every right to be damn mad about that. But, here's the key, "Be angry and *do not sin*." Ohhhh, it's how we respond to anger that can cause error. Anger exploding out or imploding in germinates into bitterness, and becomes the opportunity the enemy is looking for in which to sabotage your relationship. Don't let him, and let that tick you off so fully that you do something about it.

One thing we often overlook about Jesus is His ability to absorb the guilt. We are called to be like Him in this. Even when

---

1. Ephesians 4:25-27

He's right, He absorbs the guilt and shame in every situation. He takes the first step by taking the sin upon Himself.

When we, like Jesus, take that first step towards our spouse, we declare the space a gospel space; a safe space. This takes the power from the enemy's plan to rile us up and set us loose with emotion. This is how we get angry and don't sin. Instead of powering up, power down. Instead of inflating the situation with emotion, deflate it with surrender. Understand his tactics and you can actually use them against him.

This is excruciatingly difficult because when we're wounded, we want to wound back. Remember the heart of Christ upon the cross: "Forgive them for they know not what they do." This He said about the people that were literally killing Him. How much more can we find the gospel strength to bend this out to our spouse?

Husbands, go first on this. This simple step could be so powerful in unraveling the curse. You are to love your wives as Christ loved the church. Be like Jesus – absorb the guilt, and watch how it changes the way you conflict with your spouse.

You'd be wise to look for ways to safeguard your marriage and start setting it up for the victory promised by the gospel marriage. I want to tell you about a few tools we use to safeguard our marriage while we bend the grace of God out to each other, create a vision for our future together, and fight for our marriage.

SANCTUARY

Conflict is interesting because you don't learn how to do it while you're doing it – that's all emotion, instincts, and reflexes. We can only learn how to do it well while we're not doing it. I heard recently, "You don't learn to sail a ship in a storm." The only way to truly win the fight is to win together – by preparing when you're not in the fight. To do this, we need tools and strategies to fight well, developed, and cultivated long before the fight has even materialized.

When Jules and I were early married, one of the pastors who married us (yes, we had a few) was infamous for always getting a little too real. When his wife was around and he would say something a little shocking about their lives, she would say, "Sabo! That's sanctuary!" He would quickly stop and give an "oops" look and laugh!

After a while, Jules finally asked her what she meant by that. She explained that some things in marriage need to be safe behind sanctuary doors – only for the husband and wife to experience. We loved this and started implementing it.

Over the next few years of our marriage, as we were unraveling the curse the best we could, I noticed when we could squeeze in a date night (which was not often), it would be consumed with fighting and nagging at each other. It became infested with negativity that seeped into every other part of our lives.

I grew to secretly despise date night. This would make them more infrequent and, therefore, more intolerable as more tension would build from the lack of enjoying each other. We came to a wits' end on one date night that had been spent fighting, and in the emotion, we confessed that we didn't enjoy these anymore, vowing to either stop having them or stop using them to fight. This, of course, turned into faking it through the night because the negative emotion was still present.

That's when we came up with the idea of "**Sanctuary**."

We needed a space reserved to deal with the hard issues. We needed a space to work out the difficulties in our marriage that wasn't time we had set aside to enjoy each other.

So, every Thursday morning from 9:30-10:30, for as long as I can remember, we have had Sanctuary. It's blocked on my calendar indefinitely, and we both know it's the biggest priority of the week. Jules will even say to me, "Hey, we need to have a no-spend this week and get some money back in savings, except for Sanctuary, of course! Cool?" We go to our favorite coffee shop/breakfast spot, order four breakfast tacos and black coffee, and get down to our lists. I always let her go first. This not only saved date night, but it developed into one of the most fruitful parts of our whole marriage.

The rules are (see Appendix 1 for more on these):

Come ready to receive more than give.
Leave defensiveness at the door; armor down.
We walk out better than we walked in.
If you share it, be ready to forgive it.

Here's the profound thing about this: nine times out of ten, we can't even remember the things that drove us crazy all week. It was as if putting aside a time to talk about negative things meant only the things that really mattered made it all the way to the list! As time went on, we both started not only to enjoy sanctuary (God bless those cassava flour breakfast tacos), but we also began to look forward to it.

Now, so many couples in our sphere have started having a Sanctuary; some at night, some at a quick lunch in between their jobs, some Saturday mornings while the kids wrestle in the Chick-fil-A play area – but the fruit is all the same! Creating that space is an absolute, vision-led, God-inspired game changer.

You need an intentional space to armor down and wrestle through the journey to Christ-likeness. You need a space for conversation that you know might be negative and might have some tension. It's absolutely a necessary part of the marriage relationship, so why not do it with some strategy? I recommend implementing Sanctuary.

THE COMPOST PILE

There are issues in your marriage that stem back to childhood trauma, abuses, and really hard things your marriage is going to bring to the surface. It's part of the sanctifying work that God is doing through marriage. This is actually one of the greatest gifts of the marriage relationship, despite its difficulty. But these things can't be solved in a single fight or Sanctuary session, and so they need to be sorted through over long periods of time and with lots of wisdom and patience.

There's this analogy we read about early in marriage that has unlocked something for us. Thank you, John Piper, for this powerful tool![2]

---

2. This Momentary Marriage, John Piper

Fighting Fair

When you have a compost pile, you don't put it in the middle of the living room floor, where your kids have to step over it. You don't keep it in the kitchen where you need to prepare meals for your family. If you did, it wouldn't be long before your family becomes sick and your home turns into a dumpster! You keep it outside and away. You occasionally toss something into it, and – even more rarely – go and sift through it to see if it's become fertilizer yet. Once it has, you use it in your garden, and it becomes life and a blessing to your family. You then eat of the fruit, and your family is nourished because of it.

This is the same with these hard issues – these ten-year kind of problems. These are the childhood wounds and the hurts that you've experienced in your life and in your marriage that are too great to unravel in a night after the kids' bedtime. You need a spot for these, or they can consume your whole marriage, date nights, sanctuary, family life – they even spill into your relationship with God, *making everything sick.*

So, set them on the compost pile. They need to be dealt with, they need to be sifted through, but not every day; some not even every season. When they pop up, sift through yet again, get as far as you can, and then set it back on the compost pile. After time, as you're faithful to leave them on the pile and revisit them when needed, those huge issues will actually **become life for your marriage.** Like compost in the heap of garbage, they will turn into fertilizer for the soil of your life!

This is more fruit of being naked and without shame before your spouse.

You can be open about your shortcomings, and know your spouse is ready to fight for the new person God is creating in you. When you have a spot for those huge issues, you are communicating to your spouse that their darkness doesn't threaten you, and you love them enough to go there; that they are worth it.

I can sense when it's about time to go into our compost pile and start sifting. When the night finally comes, I will literally look Jules in the eyes, give her all my attention, and literally say, "Okay, let's go there." I want a passionate spouse, and sometimes that means we gon' fight!

The compost pile issues are the ones that usually take us out. When I talk to couples going through divorce, once we've sifted through the emotion and the nitpicky stuff they complain about, we get to some real unresolved hurt that has festered and overtaken all of the relationship.

The power of the compost pile is that you are taking the things that would destroy your relationship and turning them into fertilizer for your life. The very thing the enemy would use to dissolve the relationship can become the thing that holds it together.

CREATE SAFE PLACES TO FAIL

One of the greatest tricks of the enemy is to convince us we're better off alone and hiding our shame. That's what the fig leaf was all about after the fall.

The gospel says, "I accept you as you are, and love you too much to see you stay that way." We need a safe place to bring our shame and admit when we've made a mistake, so we can help each

Fighting Fair

other become more like Jesus. How you respond is everything. I like to think of it this way: Try to respond like the other person has something you want, not like they've taken something from you. If you respond with anger and hurt, you are teaching your spouse that they are better off hiding and lying when they make a mistake. If you respond with acceptance and forgiveness, then you are teaching your spouse that what they did is not okay, but they are better off bringing it into the light to get help. You want them to keep staying open, so respond in a way where they are more likely to keep staying open.

Speaking of safe places, I hear all the time that couples will stop a fight if their kids are around. What if we thought so strategically about our fighting styles with our spouse that we could actually pass how to "fight well" down to our kids?

What if our safe places became so safe that we can actually have some of these real disagreements with our kids in the room and pass on wisdom in conflict to them? I'm not saying that the next time the compost pile comes around you go grab your kids so they can watch your shouting match, but I am saying if they don't learn how to conflict well from you then they likely won't learn it at all.

This, of course, needs to be exercised with wisdom. Conflicts about sex and deep wounds are probably best left in the sanctuary of marriage, but conflicts about other things could be used strategically to train up our kids. Also, how differently would you think about conflict with your spouse if you had this mindset? You would literally be asking yourself, at the genesis of a conflict with your spouse, if this could be a great teaching moment for your kids and you would shift the way you had that conflict. It would inform how you conflict all around because you will **start to see the greater impact of conflict**. This would also submerge you and your spouse into the same mission for conflict, to make everything and everyone better.

FINANCES

Money is often one of the greatest sources of conflict in the marriage relationship.

Remember that Adam and Eve were the first homeless people. We are wired to crave and long for security. Jesus actually said that the love of money is the root of all evil and you cannot serve God and money.[3] It's no wonder, then, that the enemy will use the love of money to create a wedge in the marriage relationship. We need to make sure our money is a tool that serves us. We need vision on how to make sure we are its master, and that it is moving forward the legacy of our family and the kingdom of God.

Finances can also be another cool thing to get us talking. It's something that needs to be communicated about, and it's a bit easier than digging in the compost pile, or even most of the big offenses we can carry in marriage. Once there is clear communication and a common goal around finances, money will become another way to defeat your enemy and declare the gospel marriage.

Coming to a common goal with your money should start with the vision of your family. Tackling this obstacle will get communication flowing about what we want our family to be about – more on the vision for your family in Chapter 8.

---

3. Matthew 6:24

I highly recommend *Dave Ramsey's Financial Peace University*. Jules and I were living paycheck to paycheck, indebted to more credit cards than I could count, and feeling the weight and stress of all of that. This resource helped us get the tools we needed to become financially free. There are two tools in particular that really helped us gain financial freedom in our marriage and helped relieve the pressure finances can put on a marriage.

The first is the emergency fund. The idea here is that the married couple should always have at least a thousand dollars in the bank in case of an emergency. For almost every couple, this will be a reachable goal. **In marriage, you need reachable goals you can accomplish and that you can celebrate.** Not only that, but even saving just one thousand dollars and setting it in an account will give you a sense of security, showing you that you are actually able to save, and will stop the mindset of living paycheck to paycheck. Jules and I were able to do this while making very little money early in our careers in ministry.

The second is the debt snowball. The idea here is to list all of your debts and tackle them from the smallest to the biggest. Step one is to set an amount of money that goes to paying off debt. This needs to include all of your minimum payments on all of your debts and what you can go above that minimum payment. Once you have that number, you pay the minimum on all your debts, and everything extra goes to your smallest one. Once the smallest one is paid off, you take everything you were paying on that and put it to the next smallest one on top of the minimum you were already paying, and so on until all debt is paid off.

This is a strategy that sets you up to win against the interest rate game that actually makes creditors money. Did you realize the minimum payment is *actually designed* to keep you in the debt forever as the interest continues to rack up? It's only when you can pay against the principle of the debt that you can actually beat it. It also sets you up to celebrate small victories with regularity, so you stay focused, excited, and hopeful about paying off even a lot of debt.

This is a simple enough tool to get you and your spouse on the same mission and trying to complete the same goals. There are so many more tools, concepts, and strategies for making money a weapon in your arsenal. I strongly recommend Financial Peace University if you want even more.

SPEAK THE FUTURE

The Bible is consistent in that there is much power in the way we talk to each other.

Marriage is absolutely a wild journey of faith. Faith is the ability to pull God's promised future into our present reality. When I speak to my spouse, I need to speak only what pulls God's promises for her into the conversation. Don't be fooled – the enemy wishes to steal, kill, and destroy,[4] and he will use the way you speak to bring *his* desired future into *your* marriage.

We have learned to avoid, what we have been taught to call, "shotgun phrases" (I can't even remember from where). Shotgun phrases are saying things that kill the conversation. You want to learn to get a good volley going, where your spouse feels comfortable responding. We avoid language such as, *"You always... You*

---

4. John 10:10

never... Why can't you... When will you learn..." in a fight. Again, it's about declaring over them God's future.

When you say a phrase like, "*You never* hear me when I'm talking," you speak that into their future. The very phrase implies they can't change.

When you use a phrase like, "*You always push me to my limit,*" you allow the enemy's narrative to have a voice in the kind of future you are fighting for.

We try using phrases like, "*Sometimes you... I feel like you... Am I right to think...*" This leaves space for an *alternate future* to present itself; God's future. Notice that you are still fighting, and you are still dealing with the hurt, but you're **allowing space for God to change the outcome.**

Have you ever moved to a new city, started a new job, or started attending a new church, and felt like you could reinvent yourself? When people get around a new group, they realize they have an opportunity to express outwardly the change they feel has happened within. People who have been in your life for a while have a tendency to tie you to who you were, and they're so close they can't even see the change that might have occurred on the inside – especially when they get hurt. You learn from past wounds the most vividly.

We can have a tendency to lose sight that our spouse is actually changing, and **we can chain them to the past versions of themselves.**

Paul cries out in Romans, "Oh wretched man that I am! Who can save me from this body of death?"[5] In the first century, there was a death penalty where they would literally chain the offender to a decaying dead body so that, as it decayed, they would decay right along with it!

We can tend to do this with our spouses. We chain them to the old versions of themselves for so long that we can actually decay the change that took place while we weren't watching! I hate when I hear someone say, "People don't change." That is literally the whole message of the gospel! We are being changed from glory to glory from the inside out. Give space for your partner to change.

AVOID FALSE NARRATIVES

On January 8, 1815, the British marched on Louisiana, hoping to get a strategic victory in separating the lonely state from the rest of the United States. What's significant about this, is that the British and the United States had signed a peace agreement ending the War of 1812 two weeks before, but the news had not yet reached the British commander, who attacked Louisiana, and so he was still under the narrative that America was still his enemy!

This is the power of false narratives – they can spark whole wars in a season of peace.

The enemy is a master of the false narrative. Remember what he said to Eve in the garden? "You shall not eat of *any* tree in the garden?"[6] This was just a spark to ignite the flame of doubt in Eve's mind that God was good. The same happens in our marriag-

---

5. Romans 7:24

6. Genesis 3:2

es. We constantly develop narratives in our minds by reading body language, assessing whether someone is telling the truth or not, and taking the temperature of conversations. This is a subconscious and important ability that keeps us safe from bad relationships and people that might hurt us.

The problem is, sometimes, we can misread something and develop a *false narrative* – when you start to believe something about someone else incorrectly, and it seems to color everything they do. These are so powerful, in fact, that when we start to act on false narratives, it reinforces that they might be true because of how our partner responds to your reaction.

Here are a few ways to make sure you aren't developing false narratives about your spouse, and that they aren't about you:

Understand your cognitive bias – Cognitive bias is when your brain looks for information assuring you of something you already accepted as fact. This gets us into a lot of trouble. Always think critically about your own viewpoints and why you hold them. Remember, it is always better to win your spouse than to win an argument. One way this fleshes itself out all the time in my marriage is when I won't let my partner change her mind or rephrase something she said that hurt me. Sometimes, my cognitive bias tries to justify my hurt by needing my spouse to be the villain. They can rephrase a thousand times, apologize, and swear they didn't mean it that way, but to make sense of the hurt, my bias won't let it go.

In conversation, **use phrases like,** *"What I'm hearing you say is... What I feel when you act this way or say this thing is... Am I right to come to this conclusion..."* This allows your partner to control their narrative and gives them the opportunity to correct it in case you are developing a false one. When I say this to my spouse I am communicating, "This is the narrative that I'm developing; is it on track with how you feel?"

Attack false narratives. If you sense your spouse is starting to believe something that isn't true, ask them about it! The same goes if you recognize a narrative developing that might do some damage – ask your spouse for clarity. Remember, we are in a war, and we need to be in good communication if we are to take ground. Passivity will lie and say, "If you address this maybe-false narrative, then it will add forty-five minutes to the conversation." I'm telling you that forty-five minutes will pale in comparison to the damage it could wield left unchecked and uncorrected.

FIGHT OR FLIGHT

During conflict, it's important to slow emotion and try to think as rationally as you possibly can. The fall says you're programmed to react a certain way, and desire a certain outcome. The gospel says you are a new creation, and you have a new set of instincts. We can now be wise to the enemy's tactics. He will use our emotion against us so that our gut instinct that God is doing some real soul work is discarded, or he will separate our analytical brain from emotion so that we win the argument and lose the relationship.

Wisdom will point you in the direction of seeking help, but it's also important to understand what physiologically happens when you're in conflict. Our bodies are actually designed to have an instinct to lean in and *fight* or run away in *flight* when they sense danger. Mastering this can help save you from saying or doing something that will become a tool in the enemy's arsenal to destroy your marriage.

When you're in conflict, blood rushes to the back of your neck. This is what triggers your emotional fight or flight response.

Have you heard the phrase "flipping your lid"? This is when your body says it needs all of the blood in your brain, so that your instincts can take over, and you absolutely lose control of what your body does next.

This is by design to protect you in case of emergency, but a conflict with your spouse is typically not an emergency, even though all the same emotions are usually present. So, how can we trick our brain into letting us maintain control and stay strategic in a conflict?

BOXED BREATHING

Boxed breathing is practiced by Navy SEALs to regulate their adrenaline levels when they are in some dicey situations. Sometimes our marriages feel like we need to call in the SEAL team, but the reality is our partners are not our enemies so we need to trick our bodies into getting on board.

Breathe in for four seconds, hold for four seconds, spew the air out as quickly as you can, hold for four seconds, and then finally repeat as needed. What you are doing is telling your brain that your lungs need that blood and that focus.

It's always better to ask for a "time-out" than say or do something you will regret. This will lower your heart rate, give you something other than your anger or frustration to focus on, and tell your body, "You chillin', you don't need that adrenaline right now."

MUSCLE TENSING

One that really works for me is tricking my brain into thinking the blood is needed elsewhere when it's starting to rush to my head. You can't really start boxed breathing while you're at your in-laws, and Thanksgiving dinner just took a dramatic turn. We need ways to stay cool when we can't escape the tension of a hard situation.

Try this. As soon as you feel yourself start to "go there," and the blood starts to rush to your head, try flexing your calves one after the other. What you're telling your body is that your legs need the blood, not your brain.

You'd be surprised what a few tricks like this can do to your self-control in conflict. Remember – *we are in a war for our marriages*, so we, too, need to regulate these things like soldiers.

EXERCISE

We cannot underestimate the power of a healthy routine. When we are exercising regularly and eating well, our bodies metabolize some of the negative emotions that flow through us.

A Harvard Medical study in 2018 showed that physical activity can actually lower stress, anxiety, and depression, "Regular aerobic exercise will bring remarkable changes to your body, your metabolism, your heart, and your spirits. It has a unique capacity to exhilarate and relax, to provide stimulation and calm, to count-

Fighting Fair

er depression and dissipate stress."[7] Overall, a more healthier body leads to a healthier mind.

For me, the gym is a place to think hard about my marriage, kids, and legacy. Truth be told, a lot of this book was written in my mind between reps as I pondered the deep things of God. There is something about exercise that frees your mind to think about things without the normal distractions of life.

I don't even think I need to say this, but working out also enriches your sex life. When you feel good about your body, then you are more likely to have sex with your spouse. When you are having sex with your spouse, it's pretty hard to be mad at them and stay in constant conflict. Sex can be one of the greatest assets to marriage conflict because it continually ensures you are pushing to quick resolutions.

IT TAKES A VILLAGE

This is hard. There, I said it. Excruciating at times. But, you're not alone. Get help. One of the greatest things Jules and I ever did is establish relationships with older married couples that had built great marriages, after decades of putting in the hard work. Some of those relationships are as lasting as my marriage to Jules, and they still talk me off ledges to this day. And now, by God's grace, Jules and I are that sounding board for other younger couples— this is the Church being the Church!

In the teachings of Jesus, He makes it clear we need to resolve conflict quickly and easily. He even offers a method: step one, go talk to the person who has offended you. That simple truth can

---

7. Harvard Health Publishing, Published in 2011, Updated in 2018

cut off bitterness and resolve so many conflicts, but He offers a step two because He knows and understands the nature and complexities of our conflicts.

Step two: bring a few others with you. I don't know where we started to think that this is true in the church, but not in the marriage. If the marriage is the most important, and therefore most difficult and fruitful, relationship on the planet, then why doesn't this principle apply even more here? We need help. We need each other. We need people to look us in the eye and remind us that our spouse is not our enemy. We need someone to find the good in us and call it out when our spouse can't. It takes a village.

Use a sanctuary and agree on these safe people while you're not in the conflict.
The last thing you need to do is bring your best friend in on the fight when he never liked your wife anyway.

Also, discuss what information should be kept within the sanctuary of your marriage and what information is safe to share. Wisdom is found in the mouth of many counselors.[8] Don't just feed your cognitive bias by surrounding yourself with counsel you agree with. Find friends who will challenge you and point you back to your spouse. Talk with your spouse about friends you both feel comfortable opening up to and to what extent. Be wise and strategic because we are wed into a war, and the stakes are high. You are not alone, and we are so much stronger together.

---

8. Proverbs 11:14, 15:22, 24:6

THE POWER OF A COMMON ENEMY

In the end, your spouse is not your enemy.

In fact, they are designed to be your greatest ally in the fight against our actual enemy. When my wife and I turn our fight towards our actual enemy, it not only relieves us of our frustration for one another, but it actually unifies us exponentially, and you bet that's the exact opposite of what the enemy wants.

Wise up to his tactics. Jules and I have been worship leaders for a long time and started to notice that we would fight most Saturday nights – right before we needed to get sleep to be Sunday-ready. A pattern had emerged, and once we had this realization, we could pinpoint this as an attack of the enemy, and that wisdom helped us fight that attack. If we sense an argument revving up on a Saturday afternoon, we call it out and save it for sanctuary.

Understand that the enemy is after your marriage and will use a systemized and patterned attack strategy against you. Once you recognize it, his plan can't work. Understand that you have triggers and buttons that he wants to push into to get conflict going. Avoid those triggers and have wisdom in when and how you conflict.

An enemy has declared war on your marriage and on your family. Let that piss you off! Let it ignite a passion to be wise to his tactics and hold fast to your spouse. Let it be fuel to join together and defeat him and his schemes to steal, kill, and destroy what God has promised to us.

Chapter

The Gospel Divorce

What if I told you that I believe in divorce? In fact, I think every marriage should experience divorce? You'd probably call, "click bait!" And you'd be kinda right, but here's the thing – I think that marriages that *end* in divorce have divorced the wrong thing.

It's so interesting to me that guys will work, work, work, work, work (read that in "Rihanna" for me) and lose their marriages because we just can't peel away. I recently spoke with a guy who was working a second job to "pay off debt" while his marriage was crumbling. I couldn't believe it! Once that debt was paid off, and the marriage was over, he'd be stuck with an alimony payment and child support for years. His legacy would be cut off and he'd have to start over from even further behind than the last try.

The curse is a trick and a trap. It just doesn't work! I'm not saying that working two jobs to pay off debt is inherently bad or unwise, but I am saying that the gospel marriage will provide you and your spouse a launching pad to seasonally tackle every great obstacle, together, as a team.

Women do this too. She'll put the needs of her kids so far above the needs of her husband that he will either find love somewhere else, or he will shut down completely. The end of this is kids who aren't raised by both parents and a mom who is trying to fill shoes she was never intended to fill alone.

Make sure you are divorcing the right thing.
Divorce the job before you lose the wife.
Divorce the idea of being the perfect mom before you push dad out of the picture.

The marriage has to be the last thing to go! Jesus said this, "What God has joined together, let no man separate."[1] Catch the juxtaposition here? God has brought me and my spouse together. He has called the two of us, one. Man brought me the job, the stuff, the house payment, and the friends. I am not "made one" with my kids. That's just not the design. Me and my pets are not the representation of Christ and the church. It's the husband and wife that God has declared something really unique with. If divorce is on the table, or in our vocabularies, let's consider divorcing all the *other* things first.

SELF-FULFILLING PROPHECY

When I was learning how to ride a motorcycle, the instructor said something that really fascinated and stuck with me, even long after my wife had convinced me to park the bike until the kids were out of college. He said when you're on the road, the bike will steer where you are looking. If your eyes are stuck on the pothole you're trying to avoid, then that's exactly where your subconscious

---

1. Matthew 19:6, Mark 10:9

will steer the bike. If your eyes are fixed on the road and destination ahead, that's where your bike will go.

When we let the term "divorce" enter the language of our conflicts, we can actually open up an unintentional destination.

Remember, one of the enemy's tactics is to slowly allow the narrative to change so that we question the goodness and provision of God. If God is the one that has joined us with our spouse, then, of course, this is where the enemy will attack the goodness of God by asking, "Did God really have your good in mind when He gave you your spouse?" If we start to doubt that, it can actually push us into accepting divorce as an option.

The self-fulfilling prophecy is a powerful concept. It works itself out when we fear something so much that we create scenarios where it is more likely to occur. For example, if you are afraid of being cheated on, you might become paranoid about your partner, so you read through their messages, turn on "find my friends" on their phone, and hound them when you're unsure about what they are doing. This kind of behavior might suffocate them, make them slowly grow disdain for you, and eventually cause a schism in your relationship. We need to think wisely with the broken and fearful parts of ourselves, for this is exactly where the enemy will try to bring harm.

When we allow the idea of divorce to enter our conflicts, we are slowly warming to the idea that we can leave. When that becomes part of the way we communicate, even subtly, we are telling the other person to ready their hearts for us to leave. This becomes a self-fulfilling prophecy because as we ready for the other person to leave, we start to guard our hearts for their eventual departure.

When we do that we start to act as if they are thinking about leaving which gives them a reason to leave! It's a road hazard and a trap we need to steer clear of.

Divorce not only ends the marriage, but it also reinforces the curse. The men have to go work even harder than before and it reinforces the subjugation of the woman and her desire to rule the man. The idea of alimony and child support is actually a scheme to keep the woman in a place of authority over the man and to propagate the idea that the woman needs the man's money to take care of herself. It's a trick and a trap to promote the very things we despise. We also see that divorced women who have kids attach closer to those kids, reinforcing the soul-tie of the curse. This often pulls them away from their fathers and has the potential to affect children for the long-term.

If we want to achieve a great legacy and leave for our children more than what was left to us then we need to *practice* for legacy, not divorce. When we leave an argument in frustration, we are practicing to finally leave for good one day. When we allow our emotions to get the better of us, and we say things to hurt, we are actually practicing to one day finally lay it all out, no matter the body count. We are practicing for divorce. The thing we try so hard to avoid is exactly where we are pushing ourselves towards.

When we stay even though it's hard, we are practicing for legacy. We are building up *relational endurance*. When we calm our emotions and allow our new instincts to take over in speaking the gospel future to our spouse, we practice for legacy. We are practicing to build up, brick by brick, the legacy that God has for us.

The flip-side of the self-fulfilling prophecy is that it works for what God has declared over you too. When you speak as if it's coming and act as if it's here, you endure until it does.

IRRECONCILABLE DIFFERENCES

If the gospel marriage is the absolute representation of Christ and the church, then it can also be one of the greatest signs God can bring marriages on the verge of death – and even all the way dead – back to life. He takes what is broken and makes it new. That is what He does.

When married couples state "irreconcilable differences" or "too much conflict or arguing," as a recent study released as a top reason marriages end in divorce, this shows we don't understand that if the gospel doesn't work at the foundational most important human relationship you can have on Earth, then it just doesn't work. God can restore and reconcile, at the very least, in the relationship He founded to represent Christ and the church! The whole point of the gospel is every irreconcilable difference has been reconciled by and through Jesus! This reconciliation is ours in Jesus. We can claim that and speak it over our marriage relationships.

ADULTERY

Adultery, or extra-marital affairs, is one of the top reasons that people divorce, and not only that, it's the only reason Jesus talks about when referencing divorce. Let's unpack this conversation Jesus had on the subject:

"And Pharisees came up to him and tested him by asking, 'Is it lawful to divorce one's wife for any cause?' He answered,

'Have you not read that he who created them from the beginning made them male and female, and said, Therefore a man shall leave his father and his mother and hold fast to his wife, and the two shall become one flesh'? So they are no longer two but one flesh. What therefore God has joined together, let not man separate.' They said to him, 'Why then did Moses command one to give a certificate of divorce and to send her away?' He said to them, 'Because of your hardness of heart Moses allowed you to divorce your wives, but from the beginning it was not so. And I say to you: whoever divorces his wife, except for sexual immorality, and marries another, commits adultery.' "[2]

I love that this conversation happened and that it was recorded for us because the question is still being asked today, and Jesus' response is still so relevant. "What about divorce? What if there's cheating? What if there's abuse?" Jesus' response is bold, so bold that His disciples respond, "Maybe it's better to not even marry!"[3]

First, he references creation. This is important, because I want you to understand the pattern that continues through scripture around marriage. It really is a deep and lasting covenant founded from the beginning of time to tell an eternal story. That's why Jesus takes us back to pre-fall Adam and Eve, right on back to Genesis 1 and 2. **The "oneness" of marriage has always been about more than happiness.** It's about the mystery and the eternal reality of Christ and the church. This mystery wasn't even fully revealed yet, but here, Jesus is tipping His hat to it slightly.

---

2. Matthew 19:3-9

3. Check out the next verse (Verse 10)

The Gospel Divorce

Genesis is revealing even more here too. The eternally significant bond a husband has with his wife transcends the bond he has with his parents.[4] There is a *leaving* that happens with the man and his parents that juxtaposes the *staying* he does with his wife.

Our bond with our parents here is for a temporary purpose – namely raising us in stature and wisdom – while the marriage's purpose is lifelong, revealing Christ and the church. The longer a marriage stays, the more oneness we experience, and the more we are showing Christ and the church. That oneness is the great lifelong adventure of marriage, and cutting it short means we miss out on the beautiful fruit therein.

When the conversation steers towards the commandment of Moses, the Pharisees think they've trapped Jesus in an age-old debate that had been swirling in that day. This argument is still prevalent today. Sometimes, wouldn't it be better for a couple that causes more chaos together to divide for the sake of peace? Wouldn't that be the lesser evil? In my view, this is basically the main reason for divorce today. But what if God is doing so much more than choosing the lesser evil? What if He is choosing the hardest thing to shape and grow you? What if He knows I can leave the marriage, but I will still have to do this hard soul work with *someone* eventually?

Look at Jesus' response, "Because of the hardness of your heart Moses allowed you to divorce." This is interesting for a few reasons: the law is never lenient. It never relaxes because things are hard; it never bends because there's a complex situation. It is con-

---

4. It might be worth noting that the man is called to leave mother and father but there is no such calling on the woman. As I've watched marriages unfold, when the man has an unhealthy tie to his mother after marriage, it can have a pretty difficult effect on a marriage. I have seen this with women, too, but at a much less significant effect and at a much less rate.

stantly and forever showing us even our most minute of failings to push us to a deep and all-encompassing need for Jesus. So, when Moses *allowed* for divorce, it was, in my opinion, a nod to the fact that marriage transcends the law. It was always and will always be a shadow of the most gracious moment in all time, that Jesus would accept his bride, stretch out his arms in forgiveness, and declare her holy.

When Moses saw marriages around him, he saw the hardness of people's hearts. This, by the way, is the inability to escape the curse, and it's the inability to forgive. But, the gospel marriage proclaims a **new heart and instinct**, and Christ in us, which is the most powerful force in the universe. The power to forgive anything.

What I'm about to say is radical and only even possible if Jesus really died and really rose from the dead. The greatest love that we can experience, the greatest level of grace, and the greatest exponential forgiveness that we can bend out, is when there is adultery in the marriage. That is the beauty of the gospel – the darker the sin, the more lavish the grace that can be offered!

Jesus understands this, and He even "gets it" if you just can't push yourself to forgive that one. That's why he says, "Except for sexual immorality." The point is clear to me, though – *the marriage is the place where you are safest to fail, the most likely to experience the radical love and grace of God, and to be naked and without shame*. In the gospel marriage, your shame actually becomes your greatest source of life because your partner looks right at it and says, "I love you still, and I'm here to stay."

PORNOGRAPHY

The text here says "sexual immorality," and I think it's of the utmost importance that we unpack that. The Greek word is literally read, "porneia." Yep, you guessed it – the same word where we get "pornography."

This word literally means, "To sell off your sexual purity."

So, what is porn? It's anything that prostitutes our sexual purity. This shocked me to my core.

Pornography is so ugly and so dark that Jesus understands it if we just can't bring our hearts to forgive it. Forgiveness in this area is literally divine. He looks at that with so much compassion, and He sees how complex it makes the marriage relationship. He understands if the heart has not had softening required to heal here.

This word is often translated in English as "immorality" or "sexual immorality" in the Bible. That means almost every time we read "sexual immorality," we can substitute it with pornography.[5] Damn. That stings. We have expropriated this word of its power and of its utter indictment on the darkness within our hearts.

My wife was sexually abused before the age of 5 by her biological father. He was a sheriff and was therefore exposed to a lot of pornography. He claimed that this, and his own personal childhood abuse, led him to a pornography addiction that spiraled into a child pornography fascination, which in turn led him to abuse

---

5. Don't take my word for it: 1 Corinthians 5:1, 1 Corinthians 6:13, 1 Corinthians 6:18, 1 Corinthians 7:2, 1 Corinthians 7:2, Galatians 5:19, Ephesians 5:3, Colossians 3:5, 1 Thessalonians 4:3, and on through Revelation, but I want to visit that in a moment.

his children. One night, during our engagement, Jules shared this all with me, begging the question, "Where are you in your fight against porn?"

I lied. We often lie when we are more concerned with the consequences for us, than the consequences for everyone else. I decided that day to pick up a giant fig leaf, put on my "pastor hat," and say that I had complete victory over this. It didn't take long into our brand new marriage for that house of cards to come crashing down. You see, I had been battling a pornography addiction for over a decade at that point, and I had learned to lie and cover the shame of it since I was a pre-teen.

Lying about it was always my first instinct. It's how I survived adolescence and working for the church. Imagine the horror Jules went through that summer day when she discovered it on my computer. I am filled with regret and sadness even now just thinking about it.

What unfolded over the next few years was nothing short of the miracle of the gospel marriage. Jules made the choice to forgive. She saw me in my shame, all the way naked and exposed, and decided to forgive. I now understand that this choice was absolutely divine. She didn't have to. This is on the level of adultery! It's the same. We got some counselors around us, I got Covenant Eyes[6] on every device, and we began the journey to wholeness.

Honestly, this is where I learned about the power of the gospel marriage: seeing the curse unravel as my wife let go of my holiness and chose to forgive. This radically changed who I am,

---

6. A software that blocks mature content and/or also sends a report of every website that has been visited.

and I became (and still am on the wild journey of becoming) who she's always hoped I'd be.

JUST LIKE JESUS

The church, on a few occasions, is understood to have given herself over to "porneia." In fact, God's relationship with His people throughout the whole Bible is one where He forgives adultery and sexual immorality again and again. The whole book of Hosea is about how God will take back His cheating bride every time. When we forgive this, we are like God. There's really not a better way to say it. In fact, we have all been forgiven this same sin. We, ourselves, are a part of His bride that has turned to "porneia" again and again, and He forgives us, declares us new, and begins the work of rescuing our hearts. God, who has been cheated on, spat upon, beaten, and even killed, still takes his bride back. Not once was the word "divorce" on his lips. When we choose to forgive, we are like God.

UPS AND DOWNS

The battle of sex, intimacy, makes complete sense when we realize that we have an enemy that's hell-bent on destroying the marriage relationship. It's one of his most devious tactics to infiltrate into the very thing that was given to us as one of the greatest gifts of marriage. If the enemy wants to see divorce, then he will attack in the place where the human heart can't forgive. And he doesn't let up. It's an up and down journey filled with small victories and huge defeats.

Here's what the enemy doesn't understand, though – the places he hits us the hardest can develop into our places of greatest strength. When we learn to get the word "divorce" out of our vocabulary, we take the power out of our sin and thwart a major strategy of the enemy. When we lean into the gospel marriage and re-up our promise to stay, then our partner's faults have a safe place to change. Sooner or later, we all need that safe place to change, and I'm of the belief that good change happens the quickest when you can attack head-on the real issues of life in a place where you won't be judged or condemned (just like we change for the worse and develop emergency instincts in unsafe places).

MAYBE IT'D BE BETTER WITH SOMEONE ELSE

There's this Seth Rogan and Michelle Williams movie called "Take This Waltz" that kinda blew my mind about divorce. I don't really recommend the movie, and I'm about to reveal the whole plot anyway, but its message has stuck with me for years.

In the movie, Michelle's character is happily married to Seth's. They have a normal marriage, normal battles, and normal drama, but at its core, it is a happy one. Then, a new single neighbor moves in, and slowly Michelle's character is drawn to him. The whole movie watches that slow fascination germinate into a full affair. In the end, she leaves her husband to be with this new man. It's the very last shot that stayed with me in detail, even though I only watched this movie once. The camera watches them full of unrestrained passion, all over each other, finally fully giving in to their desire with nothing to hold them back. Then it spins out of frame and then back onto them, but this time there is less passion. And again, and now their life together is looking more normal. And again, and again, and again, until she is right where she started out with her last husband; on opposite ends of the couch watching TV.

This is the lie of divorce. It won't be better the next time.[7] It will start out with all the explosive affections your last marriage had, and then it will slowly take the same work. In fact, it might take more work because the scars you thought you left behind in the last marriage actually carry on to the next one, except without closure or proper healing.

FROM TWO TO ONE TO TWO AGAIN

What you have to lose is too great. That's why Jesus ends by saying that if you leave and marry someone else, you have committed adultery. You are endlessly fragmenting what God has joined together. You're no longer two people; you've been made one, and so ripping that apart means that neither side remains intact.

His literal words are "one flesh." I think He wants us to feel that "flesh" part. It's like ripping off half your body and expecting to go into another relationship. The body will need a miracle and the heart will need major surgery. You will not be the same. And this makes the next marriage pretty precarious. What parts of your last spouse are now joined to your new one and so on? Divorce is like the lie of the curse. It won't bring life, and it's not the lesser of two evils – it is the greatest evil and will steal more from you than you even knew you had to lose.

In our culture, the phrase "conscious uncoupling" has tried to soften the significance of divorce's consequences. You cannot simply uncouple just because you have both decided to. There is a

---

7. An obvious caveat is needed here. If there's abuse then this changes things drastically. Don't stay in an abusive marriage. Get help. I'm not saying that the gospel can't save it, but salvation is going to start in the community of your church and family.

spiritual reality of oneness being pulled into two in the physical. This is another lie from the enemy. Remember that he is trying to see if he can get you to agree on changing the narrative at all. He is even willing to agree that marriage is something designed by God for your wholeness, so that he can get you to give in on its intended lifespan. He's real sneaky like that.

ENABLEMENT

I am not saying that marriage is a place so safe that it enables us to stay in sinful and hurtful patterns. This is actually a good definition for the curse. The woman stays vying for control, and the man goes to work, and they miss each other like two ships in the night. **The gospel marriage is the safe place where you are fully seen and received and are moved by that acceptance to change.** The gospel marriage declares you holy and then fights like hell to get you there!

This has been my experience. Jules didn't just let me spin down into the world of pornography, but she created a safe place for me to fail, and then lovingly looked me dead in the eyes and said, in tears, that God had so much more for me. And then she embraced me. That's it right there! She loves me too much to let me stay trapped. She surrendered my holiness to God and focused on her control and fear issues, and slowly but surely we both began to find freedom and victory.

WHEN IT'S TOO LATE

This chapter might have struck at some deep hurts in your heart. I want you to know that God is in the business of restoration and resurrection. This is what He does. **He wakes what is dead to**

The Gospel Divorce

a new fierceness of life. He brings what is sick and weak into fuller strength and vitality than ever before.

The beauty of the gospel is that nothing is really dead; nothing is too far gone.

When Jules and I met Sophie, she was about to be divorced and strangely hopeful about it. Later I would find out that she had been married for eight years, and she and her husband were back together from a temporary separation when she revealed that she had been having an affair.

Her husband was so distraught that he volunteered for deployment overseas in Afghanistan and swore to divorce her. While overseas, he tried everything to get revenge and fill the void that had been left in his heart – not only from the affair, but wounds he didn't even realize he'd hoped Sophie would've healed earlier in and through the marriage.

When I was reintroduced to Gabe and Sophie, this beautiful gospel married couple, much later, I didn't realize this was *the same Sophie* that I'd met so many years earlier. It was only when they began telling their story that I realized it was the same woman.

Gabe had come home from Afghanistan feeling like it didn't even come close to healing the chasm of his broken heart, to find that Sophie had surrendered her life back to Jesus. Sophie was praying and fighting for their marriage the whole time he was gone! Gabe was shocked, and something began to stir in him. Wildly, he followed through with filing the divorce papers, then shortly after asked Sophie if they could date.

They started dating during the 90 day cool-off period Texas enforces to make sure the divorce isn't just an emotional decision. He was committed to showing Sophie he was a man of his word, so he followed through with the divorce. They made a date out of going to the courthouse and finalizing the divorce, and Gabe was hoping to hang out after, but something told Sophie that they needed space to mourn the season that just ended. This made Gabe ask a lot of questions about what he wanted and the unrealistic expectations he had put on Sophie in their marriage. During this three-month divorce period, he turned his life back to Jesus, and finally, they went on to get re-married.

When Gabe told me the story, he said, "The old marriage had to die, all the way dead, so that there could be a new covenant made between us, this time founded on Jesus." This is the gospel divorce. It is killing whatever needs to be killed to commit yourself to the oneness of you and your spouse.

And it's never too late.

Gabe and Sophie laid before each other naked and without shame, fully known and fully accepted. When they tell the story today, Gabe shares that he is thankful for the affair because the journey of forgiveness did so much work on his own soul, finally giving him what he always wanted and showing that God operates in and through the impossible.

RECONCILIATION

Reconciliation is a major theme of the gospel, but how do we actually do it when there is betrayal and trust is broken? It's an honest question and one worth asking.

The Gospel Divorce

Trust is a currency fundamental to any relationship, and once it's lost, there can be some real work to get it back. I think understanding this first is essential when trust has been broken. Trust is like a bank account in a relationship. It can take years to build up the kind of relational equity that trust affords, and it can be depleted in a second.

The difficult thing about betrayal is that it makes the person who has been betrayed doubt the whole worldview they have sculpted in the time they were with the betrayer. They are forced to, at a fundamental level, question everything. The damage this does to the human heart and psyche is so potent that it's the only reason Jesus is even willing to broach the topic of divorce. More on that in the next chapter, but I do want to highlight here that as trust is rebuilt and the journey of forgiveness begins, there will be conflict.

At the beginning of reconciliation, there has to be what I call a "nucleus of truth."

The problem with lying and betrayal is that once I have betrayed, the narrative that I am a liar starts to take shape, and trust has been lost. Everything that comes out of my mouth after the betrayal is a maybe-lie, and, therefore, is about as good as a lie. For the journey of reconciliation to begin, there has to be a nucleus of truth, a collection of facts the betrayer and betrayed can agree on as truth.

If the betrayer continues to hold on to more details of their innocence that the person who is hurt can't accept, then you can't start the journey. Likewise, if the person who has been hurt demands for the betrayer to accept more than they are guilty of, and they won't, the journey can't begin. If we can't agree on a starting line, we can't start the race.

Once we have this nucleus of truth, healing can begin and trust can start to rebuild. Like small deposits into a bank – slow at first, then exponential. Trust can start to add up again. I think understanding this process frees the betrayed to understand why there is no trust and helps the betrayer understand why it's taking so much time.

When we have a vision for what reconciliation might take, it gives us the energy to endure the long process of rebuilding. The next two chapters will deal heavily on how to heal from sexual sin and more on reconciliation from betrayal.

Confession is essential to reconciliation and healing from a marriage that has been tattered by betrayal. There has to be a safe place for confession by the one who has been hurt, and quick and truthful confession from the betrayer. I know this journey well.

When I'm caught instead of confessing, then my relational debt becomes greater, and finally, with enough of those stacking up, my debt becomes insurmountable. This will lead to the inevitable death of my relationship. When I confess, however, no matter how much I think it will hurt more than if I didn't, I am actually depositing into the relational savings that I am trying to rebuild.

I'M NOT ON MY FIRST

I understand there may be a few readers who are not on their first marriages. I can't even understand the complexities you've endured, and I truly applaud the courage you've had to make

The Gospel Divorce

it this far in the book. Make this one count. Just because you've failed doesn't mean it's too late. Love your spouse like Christ does the church, and recover what's been stolen from you! Put into practice the things you've learned here and elsewhere, and bend the grace of God to your spouse with more zeal than ever before. Failure can actually be the great catalyst to learned success.

A FEW MORE THINGS

The second marriage divorce rate is higher than the first, and even exponentially higher for third marriages, and so on. Practice doesn't make perfect because you're practicing for the wrong thing. When you leave, you're practicing for divorce. You're practicing for the "I can't do this anymores" and the "I've had all I can takes." You'll likely retreat more quickly the next time.

You go into your next marriage with more baggage and less assets. Divorce will leave you broke and broken-hearted. You will be more set up to fail than you were when you started the last marriage.

Divorce is a lie and a trap designed to make us generationally poorer, both spiritually and fiscally. We build equity in our lives when we stay with our partner, and divorce would see that equity surrendered and divided, which leaves the generations of our legacy at a deficit.

The whole idea of the gospel marriage is that we pass on generational spiritual and fiscal wealth to establish our children in strength so they can continue the war for God's Kingdom with a better start than we had. When the enemy brings divorce into that legacy, he castrates its power, and it will take a few generations to recover – more on this in Chapter 8.

Divorce tries to sabotage legacy. Children of divorce are fifty percent more likely to get married to another child of divorce. Some studies have shown that daughters of divorced parents have a sixty percent higher divorce rate than children of non-divorced parents, while sons have a thirty-five percent higher rate. We pass to our kids what we cannot overcome. This is a law of the universe that God set us in.

Malachi speaks soberly about the effects of divorce on our kids.

"Because the Lord was witness between you and the wife of your youth, to whom you have been faithless, though she is your companion and your wife by covenant. Did he not make them one, with a portion of the Spirit in their union? And what was the one God seeking? Godly offspring. So guard yourselves in your spirit, and let none of you be faithless to the wife of your youth. 'For the man who does not love his wife but divorces her, says the Lord, the God of Israel, covers his garment with violence, says the Lord of hosts. So guard yourselves in your spirit, and do not be faithless.'"[8]

We will discuss this further in chapter eight, but the fruit of the gospel marriage is godly offspring. It's what God was after when He created Adam and Eve. That's why Malachi takes us back to pre-fall here – divorce puts this in great jeopardy. That is why Malachi tells us here, when there's divorce, we have covered our garment with violence.

---

8. Malachi 2:14-16. This is actually a quite sobering account of one of the reasons God rejects worship. That's how powerful divorce is!

The Gospel Divorce

This is a weird statement to us here in the west, but what I believe the author is warning us of, is when divorce enters the family, the covering of blessing marriage is intended to be, is compromised. It puts a weak link in the chain of our lineage that can be exploited by the enemy, and it makes our places that need healing even more susceptible and open to attack.

Marriage is the covering of blessing. It covers our weaknesses while offering them wholeness and healing. It swallows up our faults ensuring they are not passed onto future generations. It's the great launching pad of legacy and wisdom. As long as we fight to stay married, we keep the blessing of God's provision upon us.

I love how Malachi shows us when we are joined to our spouse there is an extra portion of His Spirit upon the union. This is before the moment that the Spirit of God was poured on all men at Pentecost. This is even before Jesus! The Spirit of God is accessible in your marriage. He is near and ready to empower!

Another translation of this passage reveals that God hates divorce[9], and once we see its destructive power we should too. Under the cover of God's blessing, and with extra Holy Spirit, God seeks to bring forth godly offspring. Why? Because godly offspring produce godly offspring that produce, you guessed it, godly offspring. This is how heaven comes to earth! One family at a time. One marriage at a time. Divorce compromises that for a few generations and the reality of heaven on earth is again slowed. We must fight to stay.

---

9. NASB reads, "For I hate divorce," says the LORD, the God of Israel..."

THE UNBELIEVING SPOUSE

I can't imagine how difficult it might be to read this book if you have a spouse who doesn't follow Jesus. I applaud your courage and the radical faith to make it this far. The power of the gospel marriage doesn't ignite simply because of belief. Marriage is a picture of Christ and the church, whether or not the couple follows Jesus. If you think about staying with an unbelieving spouse, it's quite beautiful.

God has chosen humanity's deepest love for one another to show how much He loves humanity. The fact that you are bending gospel love, grace, and acceptance to someone who doesn't understand how to bend it back is possibly the most radical gospel love that can be shown. That's Jesus-like radical love. He died for people who didn't even believe in Him.

Paul, in his wisdom, put it this way,

"If any brother has a wife who is an unbeliever, and she consents to live with him, he should not divorce her. If any woman has a husband who is an unbeliever, and he consents to live with her, she should not divorce him. For the unbelieving husband is made holy because of his wife, and the unbelieving wife is made holy because of her husband. Otherwise your children would be unclean, but as it is, they are holy. But if the unbelieving partner separates, let it be so. In such cases, the brother or sister is not enslaved. God has called you to peace. For how do you know, wife, whether you will

The Gospel Divorce

save your husband? Or how do you know, husband, whether you will save your wife?"[10]

The word *holy* here is simply conveying that when we bring Jesus around anybody, they are set apart for His purposes. When you bring Jesus into your home, even if you are the only one doing it, then Jesus lives there too, and His influence is undeniable.

Never underestimate the power of being like Jesus to those who don't believe. And I really mean that – be like Jesus. The Jesus who laughed and drank and lived life with sinners. He didn't come condemning; He found joy in being in the presence of humanity because He loved it whether or not they knew who He was. His presence alone was enough to change hearts and save the most hopeless of people. You bring Him into your home when you are like Him! Everyday you stay, you show gospel love, and that gospel love's influence will not be in vain.

THERE IS AN END GOAL

Think about your hardest fight with your spouse. Think about the emotions that you felt during that fight, and redirect them to everything trying to steal your marriage from you. Divorce is a lie, and I'm sick of it. I'm mad at the idea that people are walking around full of shame, believing if they get real then their spouse will leave. They are in prisons and isolation, feeling unloved, unseen, and unfulfilled.

---

10. 1 Corinthians 7:12-16. It's worth noting that Paul actually breaks from Holy Spirit inspired writing here to give some advice he believes is wisdom. That's why the verse begins with the parenthetical, "I, not the Lord" statement. This is cool because he understands the true complexity of being married to someone who doesn't believe. It's so intricately complex that he wasn't even sure if he had the mind of God on the matter. I think this means that this can be taken case by case and walked with multiple counselors and lots of prayer.

I'm ready to see the gospel marriage set hearts free! I'm ready to see man be what he was created to be; naked and unashamed journeying deep into the heart of the wild and unknown frontier of his wife. I'm ready to see the woman be what she was created to be: naked and unashamed, journeying into the wild adventure that is her husband.

In Matthew 22, the religious leaders of Jesus' day try to trick Him by asking which man gets the woman who's been married seven times in heaven. This was a mystery up until Jesus answered them. He makes this really interesting statement: "For in the resurrection they neither marry nor are given in marriage, but are like angels in heaven."[11]

Marriage is a lifelong journey with eternal implications. It is a race you can finish and finish well. The fruit is unimaginable joy, legacy, acceptance, and divine love. You would be wise to run and to run well after your spouse all the days of your life because *there is a finish line,* and you've got what it takes to get there!

Marriage is for the journey of life on Earth, but its effect echoes into eternity.

---

11. Matthew 22:30

The Gospel Divorce

Chapter

Let's Talk About Sex

Sex is the pinnacle of physical oneness in the marriage relationship and is itself a symbol of what God has done in our hearts in making us one with our spouse.

It is also one of the marriage's greatest weapons. It keeps your marriage young at heart and healthy in spirit. The enemy knows this, and that is why he attacks this spot aggressively. We saw in the last chapter that the very thing given to the marriage to safeguard it and celebrate it is the very place the enemy uses to divide us and push us to the precipice of divorce. The fact of the matter is, God intended this to be a safe haven of the marriage, a wellspring that brings life and flourishment through the marriage, and, therefore, it has the biggest target on it.

We live in a world where sex in the context of anything *but* marriage is celebrated. The enemy has done well to make sure that sex within marriage is viewed as dull, monotonous, and awkward. God has everything but that in mind for your sex lives.

Just read what He has to say about sex in the Song of Solomon,

"I came to my garden, my sister, my bride, I gathered my myrrh with my spice, I ate my honeycomb with my honey, I drank my wine with my milk."

Then God literally turns to the married couple and says, "Eat, friends, drink and be drunk with love!"[1] This is about as sensual as you can get. I almost want to unpack the myrrh, spice, honeycomb, and wine, but I'll just say that it all means the wildest thing you can think, and I'll leave it there.

God literally says, "Be drunk with love. Let it intoxicate you. Be wild in it. Enjoy your spouse, and enjoy them in fullness all the way to complete satisfaction."

This chapter is not going to be the "Nine Tips to Get His Engine Revving" or "Do the Dishes and She'll Do Anything!" kind of chapter. There are plenty of books on tips for a better sex life. What I want this chapter to be, rather, is an in-depth look at what sex is designed to be in the gospel marriage. We will examine a few passages on the matter and see how the act of sex was a prophetic declaration of Christ and the church even since before Jesus walked in the flesh.

FIRST LINE OF OFFENSE

Sex was created to be a recalibration tool for our marriage. The game is rigged – the woman wants it when she's been loved; the man wants it when he's been respected. By design, we don't get

---

1. Song of Solomon 5:1

it the way we want it until we put all our focus, effort, and strategy into loving our spouse. It's the reward when we live into the gospel marriage. The gospel marriage actually promises great and frequent sex! It's this way so that our sex life cannot flourish as long as the curse dominates our marriage relationship.

Sex constantly pushes us back to each other and back to Jesus. It keeps us grounded on the grace that is promised through the gospel marriage. It is designed to keep us right where God wants us.

I can't express enough how important sex is to unraveling the curse. "Oneness" is at the center of the purpose of marriage. That's why we've already seen Moses, Jesus, and Paul reference, "The two shall become one flesh." This is a central theme of the gospel marriage. This is a central theme because it points to the eternal reality that Jesus is becoming one with His bride, the church.

Sex is the physical act of declaring war for spiritual oneness. Paul tells us right after the gospel marriage chapter[2], "We do not wrestle against flesh and blood, but against the rulers, against the authorities, against the cosmic powers over this present darkness, against the spiritual forces of evil in the heavenly places."[3] I'll bet you've never heard that verse in the context of sex! It's one of our greatest weapons in the physical to do battle in the spiritual. Every time we come together with our spouse, we prophesy that love wins in the end, that Jesus has come for His bride, and that He will complete the oneness promised to us.

---

2. Ephesians 5

3. Ephesians 6:12

Sex was designed to be a celebration of marriage! When sex in the marriage becomes a celebration, then it becomes a reaffirming of the covenant made, a battle strategy in the war for God's kingdom come, and an assault on our enemy! When the canon of the scriptures was laid out they put the most sensually graphic book right in the middle of the Bible. Song of Solomon paints a rather vivid picture of the celebration of sex in the marriage[4], and Solomon wasn't even done there! He also writes in Proverbs, "Rejoice in the wife of your youth, a lovely deer, a graceful doe. Let her breasts fill you at all times with delight; be intoxicated always in her love."[5]

If sex is full of shame, miscommunication, and unfulfillment, you're doing it wrong. That wasn't the design, and my prayer is that God would open your eyes to what He always had in mind with your gospel sex life.

It might be worth noting that sex has been equated with drunkenness a few times. This is an interesting metaphor for sure. Alcohol has gotten quite a bad reputation in religious circles. I don't want to downplay the negative effects of alcohol mixed with foolishness, but we get this idea from really only one verse in the Bible.

In his book to the Ephesians, Paul makes the comment, "Do not be drunk with wine for it is useless, but be filled with the Spirit."[6] This isn't even a command; it's a metaphor. Paul isn't say-

---

4. If you don't believe me go check out Song of Solomon chapter 4 and 5

5. Proverbs 5:18–19

6. Ephesians 5:18. I understand that there may be a few more verses about Paul not wanting anything but Jesus in control of his mind or body. I find these arguments pretty thin because sex is equated with drunkenness. If he were talking about substances taking control, then he would also forbid sex.

ing, "alcohol is bad." He's saying that it's useless *in comparison to* being filled with the Spirit. He's saying that as obvious as it is when you're drunk, is how obvious that it should be when you're filled with the Spirit of God. People can tell when you're filled with spirits, so they should be able to tell when you're filled with the Spirit. This thought was never intended to condemn alcohol.

Throughout the scriptures alcohol is used as a symbol of celebration and prosperity[7]. Jesus affirms this idea again and again through his ministry. He even makes the best wine for a wedding where the guests were already pretty tipsy. He got the reputation of a drunkard because of who He drank with. You don't get that reputation without at least a little bit of effort!

Jesus makes this comment in the gospels responding to the question of why His disciples don't fast: "Can the wedding guests fast while the bridegroom is with them? As long as they have the bridegroom with them, they cannot fast."[8] Where Jesus is and where His presence saturates, there will be a party, and sometimes there will be drinking at that party!

What I am saying here is that alcohol can be a gift to your marriage if consumed responsibly and in seasons of joy. Alcohol becomes a problem when it is used to numb the pain of a hard season, enabling you to avoid the soul work that God is doing. I like to say that I drink because I'm happy, not to get happy. Alcohol can be a powerful tool to enrich the marriage bed and remind us of the joy of being together. Have a few drinks, and enjoy the gospel marriage work that Jesus is doing in and through you. Cheers!

---

7. Proverbs 3:9-10, Deuteronomy 7:13, 11:14, 33:28, Judges 9:13, Psalm 104:14-15, Isaiah 62:9 and that's not even half of them!

8. Mark 2:19

THE GOSPEL SEX LIFE

In his letter to the church at Corinth, Paul shows us that biblical oneness was also always really about Jesus. He says, "The body is not meant for [porneia] but for the Lord, and the Lord for the body."[9] He goes on to unpack that the physical act of sex brings the spiritual reality of oneness. He even references, "the two shall become one flesh" from the creation account and calls us to "flee [porneia]"[10] because it attacks the very fabric of our personal sexuality. It is an assault on our own bodies, confusing gender and the place that was created to be the most sacred. More than that, [porneia] is an assault on the deeper and hidden reality of sex.

Sex is the symbolic metaphor of the oneness that Jesus longs for with His bride, and that expression is only holy and authentic in the context of the marriage relationship.[11] He ends this section by saying this phrase, "You are not your own, for you were bought with a price. So glorify God in your body."[12] This is the stage he sets before he goes into some thoughts about the gospel sex life. You are not your own. Keep that in mind as we unpack this passage:

---

9. 1 Corinthians 6:13

10. 1 Corinthians 6:18

11. 1 Corinthians 6:16b-17 says it this way: "For, as it is written, 'the two shall become one flesh.' But he who is joined to the Lord becomes one spirit with him." There is a deep and mysterious concept to be thought through here; perhaps the eternal purpose of the physical act of sex. I am absolutely not saying or implying that Jesus longs for the act of sex with the church, but I am saying there is a mystery here, hidden in God and not yet fully known or understood. Paul is alluding here to a deeper and more spiritual revelation: that in the same way we experience oneness through the act of sex, we can be have oneness with God.

12. 1 Corinthians 6:19b-20

"Because of the temptation to [porneia], each man should have his own wife and each woman her own husband. The husband should give to his wife her conjugal rights, and likewise the wife to her husband. For the wife does not have authority over her own body, but the husband does. Likewise, the husband does not have authority over his own body, but the wife does. Do not deprive one another, except perhaps by agreement for a limited time, that you may devote yourselves to prayer; but then come together again, so that Satan may not tempt you because of your lack of self-control."[13]

The word "porneia" is all over these thoughts from Paul. I took the liberty of switching out "sexual immorality" with "porneia" so we can start to let this word bear its weight.[14]

This passage is so often read in a neutral connotation, like, "So that you don't lust after things, get a wife," when in reality, Paul is saying so much more. Marriage is supposed to be on the offense against the prostitution of our purity. Another way to say it is that sex is our greatest weapon against pornography. So often we think about this backwards. Don't miss the contrast here. Paul is saying, "The temptation of selling out your sexual purity is everywhere and in abundance, so have your *one and own* [spouse]." There is a beauty in sharing this with the one and only designed to hold it for you, and that singular expression of sex will guard your sexual purity.

Sex actually makes you pure when it's with your spouse. How beautiful is that? Not only that, but look at what else Paul

---

13. 1 Corinthians 7:2-5

14. I have used brackets to signify when switching "sexual immorality" with "porneia."

says here: there is a design for your sex life. It was meant for your *own* spouse. In contrast to porneia being everywhere and in abundance, cheap and dirty, there is a right, true, and clean way. When was the last time you thought about your relationship with sex, and the word "clean" popped into your head? This is the promise of the gospel marriage.

I love what Paul says in the next sentences. Your body is your spouse's, and their body is yours. It's out of the gospel flow of mutual submission that the curse is unraveled, and the marriage bed flourishes.

We undo the curse with mutual submission, and then declare it has no more hold on us when we have sex! This was *radical thinking* for the first-century mind. For the man to have authority over the woman was the cultural norm, but this proves the point that the gospel has much more in mind for gender roles when it says that the woman has authority over the man's body! The gospel marriage unravels the curse and places woman as she was created – at man's side.

We make much of Jesus and what He's accomplished on our behalf when we make love with our spouse. The husband declares the unraveling of the curse when he gives the authority over his body to his wife. This kind of gospel thinking will give you and your spouse a vision for your sex life, and that vision can be a fuel and weapon to help you fight for it. Remember, too, that we started out with, "you are not your own." The mutual submission of authority of our bodies to each other flows out of surrendering that authority to God. He has bought us back and redeemed us for a purpose: displaying Christ and the church through our gospel marriages and sex.

Let's Talk About Sex

Sex should be like food for you marriage. You need it with regularity, and, like food, it is best when you put time and thought into cultivating it. It should be part of your communication constantly (great sanctuary topic of conversation by the way) as it is your weapon of warfare in this battle we find ourselves in, and can be easily twisted and manipulated to bring exactly the opposite of what it was designed to.

If and when you do take a break from sex, heed the wisdom of Paul here, "Do not deprive one another, except perhaps *by agreement* for a limited time." I have seen too many couples go countless weeks without getting any, or even talking about the subject! I love that this is in the Bible because I believe that one of the best things we can do for our sex lives is to actually talk about it with our partners, openly and honestly. This conversation about how long we wait between sessions is so wise to simply get us talking. I think it's a brilliant starting place, and once we've established good dialogue around this concept, it will open doors to talk about the other intricacies of marriage and relationships.

If you do break, there's really only one good reason for it: to pray! I love that so much; four days between sessions and all I'll be doing is praying! This may seem rigid or a bit legalistic, but hear the heart behind what Paul is saying – ***the gift of sex is too great, and it's a weapon too valuable to be exchanged for anything that is not a greater weapon.*** That's right, folks – Paul puts sex right next to prayer in the fight for your marriage. Tell that to your community group!

Paul understands that the enemy is after our sexual purity, and that's why he ends this section by calling Satan out by name. Satan is always using the coward's way to attack us, which is why he seems to edge himself in when we are at our weakest and most vulnerable. Understand that long times between sex with your spouse is exactly what he's looking for to strike at the marriage covenant. Be wise to his methods, and dialogue with your spouse about how to safeguard your sex life and purity.

I understand that it can be so awkward to talk about. Have you ever thought about why that is? Could it be that this is one of the lies of the enemy? I mean, think about it – we have sex with our spouse, which is about as open and vulnerable as you can be with another person, but for some reason just talking about it with that same person is so much harder than the act itself.

Satan is happy to let the topic of sex sit in no-man's-land so we don't have a healthy dialogue about it, and he can keep informing the narrative. It's okay to own that you lack self-control and allow the marriage to influence your purity. It's no fool who allows their spouse to join them in the fight for their purity. It's time for us to strategize together for our purity, in the fight against porneia, and establish a healthy dialogue about our sex lives.

NAKED AND UNASHAMED

Sexual purity is a target because it is the central issue of the fall of man. The first thing Adam and Eve did after the fall was to hide their sexual identities. This has swung us into the chaos of sexual and gender confusion. The gospel marriage wishes to reclaim our gender and sexuality by unraveling the curse and presenting us naked and unashamed before our spouse. This is a radical idea when we understand it practically. The gospel marriage says she can accept him as fully man, with all of the desires and gravitas that it is to be man. The gospel marriage says he can accept her as fully woman, with all of the strength and beauty that it is to be woman. It proclaims that your fetishes can be known and celebrated, that the darkest parts of your sexuality can be redeemed and restored. It promises that your sexual wounds can be healed. This is what it means to be naked and unashamed.

Speaking of the gender and sexual confusion of our day, could it be that the marriage has been emasculated of the glory of our gender and the power of our sexuality, and so the world has to look elsewhere? This is the tragedy of the curse. Marriage is a joke, because we are fixated on the wrong things – babies and work, babies and work, babies and work! What would it look like for the man to put all of his energy into wooing and adoring his wife? Going into that wild frontier and making her want him? What would it look like for the woman to celebrate him for all that he is instead of fixating on what he's yet to be? I think there would be a new and indisputable power in the marriage that would correct the narrative and bring back the efficacy of our genders.

Sex was designed for marriage because oneness was designed for marriage. This is because marriage isn't about sex – it's not even about us; it's about Christ and the church. As my pastor, Rob Koke, put it: sex is the fire of your life, marriage is the fireplace. Take that same fire and put it anywhere else in your home, and it becomes absolutely destructive. But in the fireplace, it is life for your whole house.

Sex is not only safe within the covenant that promises to cover shame, but it becomes warmth, passion, and fuel for your entire life. Taking sex out of the covenant is what has made confusion of its meaning and sanctity today.

THE HONORABLE MARRIAGE

The word "intimacy" is a hot topic for marriage these days. Intimacy can actually be defined as "naked before your spouse and without shame." The effect of true intimacy goes way past the bedroom, outside your marriage, and sets you on the trajectory to be the most gospel dangerous version of your true self.

When you have total intimacy with your spouse you are in a safe place to grow, and you also stand strong in who you know God has empowered you to be.

Sexual intimacy is the physical acceptance of your spouse, and the spiritual promise and declaration to stay through until the end of what God has started with them. It is not merely the reward and passion of the relationship, but it is the ever-present reminder that God is not done yet and that He is absolutely faithful. It's also the reminder we all need to equip us to keep staying, keep standing, and keep fighting for our families.

I keep fighting because I know my spouse is proud of who I am and is committed to me until I am who I'm becoming. She proves this is true because of what happens in the bedroom. She re-ups the promise three to five times a week! And I'm telling you, it is fire under me to continue the work God has started, and it reminds me of who I am when I need to go kick butt at work, church, and in life.

Towards the end of the book of Hebrews, there is this great verse: "Let marriage be held in honor among all, and let the marriage bed be undefiled."[15] Marriage is to be honored, and the

---

15. Hebrews 13:4

impetus of that honor is the marriage bed. Catch the contrast here. What happens in the marriage bed – which is the holy and hidden place of the marriage – propels the marriage into the atmosphere of the honorable for all the world to see. If the marriage bed is defiled by shame, or sin, or the lies of the enemy, then the marriage loses its honorability in the world.

The honorable marriage has a vibrant and full sex life that is the epicenter of true intimacy in the marriage. In a culture where sex is so confused, the gospel marriage is to be esteemed because the world needs to see it in its fullness of design and power! I can't even tell you how important this actually is.

I've noticed that my own marriage with Jules has already been such a light to those we walk with. How amazing is that, considering how our journey has been through so much brokenness in the area of sexual sin? That's what God does through the gospel marriage: He takes what is broken and restores it so that all may know He brings life from the dead, and He finishes what He starts.

I think it's pretty cool that the writer of Hebrews puts these two ideas together: **honor and sex.** I think I've made a pretty good case for the gospel marriage to be worthy of honor amidst an unbelieving world, but how shocking is it that our gospel marriage sex life should also stand with honor?

Our sex lives are beacons of hope. It is the full physical expression that Jesus will be made one with His bride, the church. It is the promise that what God has begun with the church He will consummate. The gospel sex life actually reminds us and declares to the world that God will complete what He has started in our own hearts.

I mean, just think about the beauty of sex. For a moment, everything stops, and joy is all there is. In that timelessness, you are one with God, and God is one with you. It is the expression of the promise of the future of the church in Christ.

The marriage bed is undefiled. This word "undefiled" is the same word used earlier in the book of Hebrews where it describes Jesus, "We should have such a high priest, holy, innocent, *undefiled*, separated from sinners, and exalted above the heavens."[16] The marriage bed is holy. It is that sanctified and set-apart place of our marriage. The enemy has done well to make it a place of shame, secrecy, hidden brokenness, and confusion. The fact is, though, that God has called it undefiled the same way Jesus is undefiled. We need to guard it as such. We need to discuss with our spouse what parts need to stay hidden and sacred, and what parts need to be expressed and used to help others. It is a great tactic of the enemy to bring shame into the marriage bed – how we talk about it either places confidence or shame there.

Sex can be a great motivator. I have seen people do crazy things to get it; heck, I do crazy things to get it! One thing that is interesting to me is that when people get divorced, they will change all of their bad habits that ruined their marriage so they become a "marketable" version of themselves again and find a new mate.

Why not allow gospel marriage sex and, more importantly, the legacy that God is promising through the gospel marriage to motivate us now?

---

16. Hebrews 7:26, emphasis added

Why not look at some of the bad habits that are slowly decaying our marriages, and make some aggressive changes to them now so that we might awaken our marriages?

You have so much more to gain if you do, and so much more to lose if you don't. This is the gospel divorce. Divorce the TV. Divorce Netflix. Divorce the damn carbohydrates if you have to! Save the marriage.

I mentioned this in the fight chapter, but get your butt to the gym. Seriously. Get up right now and go. Get that sexy back *for your spouse*. For your marriage. For the sake of the gospel. Put this book down and go get your heart rate to something above what it gets to when you hit one flight of stairs. Heck, take the book, just go!

The fruit of getting your whole body and mind healthy again can literally save your marriage and be another building block in establishing your legacy. Not only does exercise metabolize some of those negative thoughts and emotions, but it builds back up your self-discipline. With self-discipline comes the ability to resist the enemy and to get your fight back for your marriage.

I don't know when we became okay with getting in shape to get our spouse, and then thinking now that we're in the war for marriage, we can become lazy and lax on our physical and mental presence. We need to be stronger and more focused than ever. We are in a war!

THE FRUIT OF THE GOSPEL MARRIAGE

God, in His infinite wisdom, has chosen that sex is how we get kids. I know, you weren't expecting this level of scientific and biological analysis from this book, so you're welcome.

They are the fruit, and they continue to be fruit as we raise them out of the overflow of the gospel marriage – more on that in chapter eight. It's worth noting that God literally designed sex to be life-giving. Literally. Your sex life is not only designed to bring forth literal life into the world, but the spiritual life of joy, strength, and hope into an otherwise hopeless world.

Let's Talk About Sex

Chapter

Unraveling the Past

So, here's where we left off with Adam and Eve. They're unemployed. They're homeless. They're missionless.

Their relationship is now experiencing sin and brokenness. Perhaps, worst of all, they're disconnected from God and the promise of His legacy. They're confused about who to believe. They ate the fruit, and they didn't die, so was the enemy telling the truth? But there is also the fact that they're fully aware of the new reality of shame and nakedness. Was God telling the truth? Now what?

Well, they have sons. When Cain kills Abel, it is the first moment to reveal that Satan had in fact, been lying, that God had given them the choice of God or not-god for a very real reason and death had certainly entered the world through the fall. This had to be one of the hardest things for Adam and Eve to go through.

The consequence of Adam and Eve choosing not-god was literally one of the worst pains humanity could experience in this life. Still, today, the loss of a child cannot be compared to. Not only that, but catch the gravity of what's going on here. Remember that God had snuck in the promise of Jesus within the curse, "[Eve's] offspring will crush [the enemy's] head and [the enemy] shall bruise [her son's] heal."[1] When Eve had her first son, Cain, she *had* to be thinking that finally, her seed would defeat her enemy and restore to them all that they had lost. That's why the Genesis account shows Eve saying, "I have gotten a man with the help of the Lord."[2] This "man" was supposed to crush the head of the snake. Unfortunately, Cain doesn't crush the head of the enemy – he crushes his brother's.

Cain had issues he was born into that had a real effect on the way he saw himself and the world. When it came time for him to give worship to God, we can see that his heart was confused by identity issues from the fall. Sometimes, when a mother ties to the soul of her kids she can put a burden of becoming on them so overwhelming that their spirit is strangled by it.

Cain was expected to crush the enemy. This is a burden that was not his to carry, and it weighed on him. When you can't live up to the expectations of those closest to you, especially the ones you're designed to look to for guidance and self-worth, you are constantly trying to figure out who you are and what brings you worth.

---

1. Genesis 3:15

2. Genesis 4:1. It is also worth noting that you can see the development of the soul tie here. Eve overlooks the man God had given her already, Adam, unto the son as the man she needed. Adam is actually the one who "helped" her conceive Cain, but she gives credit to God who actually literally brought to her Adam. All very interesting.

Not only that, but his job was to grind up against the curse and bring fruit from the ground. We see in Genesis that he "brought to the Lord *an* offering of the fruit of the ground, and Abel also brought *of the firstborn* of his flock."[3] Cain brought what could be replaced, and not the best he could offer, while Abel brought forth something that could not be replaced and was foreshadowing of the gospel.

Cain's offering, combined with Cain's response to that offering being rejected is indicative of his heart posture in offering it. It wasn't worship, it was self-medication. Cain was broken because he was raised by broken parents. I am broken, because I, too, have been raised by broken parents.

The gospel marriage has been perfectly designed to journey into the nuances of your past and childhood wounds, identify the places you've been broken, and provide wholeness and healing to those areas. If you think about it, you spend twenty or thirty-something years learning how to navigate around that brokenness and develop coping mechanisms to survive, and then you're joined with your spouse for sixty years to unpack all that brokenness and achieve true wholeness.

God understands the complexities of the hurts we carry, and the gospel marriage provides that safe place, that person who looks your shame in the eyes and still says, "I'm not going anywhere." That's why we have concepts like "the compost pile" from chapter four. Some traumas we experience along the way need *decades* to heal, and only in a place where we have *unmerited and irrevocable belonging*. This journey, though excruciatingly difficult, can become light and life for your marriage and family.

---

3. Genesis 4:3-4, italics added

The curse would say to blame your spouse and their family for their deficiencies and past wounds, but the gospel says to claim your role in bringing healing and wholeness to those areas. Blame or claim. Cain had God step in to preserve his legacy[4], but it was only after he was able to face what he had done and the path the curse had set him on.

This was a powerful thought for me. I sit at a fork in the road every day with the option to blame my wife's family for all the trauma they have been a part of, or to realize that I am now a part of that family and can claim the responsibility to be a part of the healing that God will eventually bring. *Once you claim your role in the story of the gospel's redemption of your new family, you are the changing variable the enemy didn't expect*, working from the inside to see the gospel do its work.

When you take the stance of blame, you remain on the outside, where the enemy wants you. When you claim your role as a healer, then God can, and will, heal through you.

THE GOD OF ALL COMFORT

That's why Paul writes in his second letter to the church at Corinth:

"Blessed be the God and Father of our Lord Jesus Christ, the Father of mercies and God of all comfort, who comforts us in all our affliction, so that we may be able to comfort those who are in any affliction, with the comfort with which we ourselves are comforted by God. For as we share abundantly in Christ's sufferings, so through Christ we share abundantly in comfort too. If

---

4. Genesis 4:15

we are afflicted, it is for your comfort and salvation; and if we are comforted, it is for your comfort, which you experience when you patiently endure the same sufferings that we suffer. *Our hope for you is unshaken, for we know that as you share in our sufferings, you will also share in our comfort."*[5]

The idea here is that the husband is receiving grace, acceptance, and comfort from God, and then bending it out to his spouse while the wife is receiving grace, acceptance, and comfort from God and bending it right back. This is how we make the necessary environment to travel deep into those calloused wounds and finally bring real healing.

Remember, the church is a family made up of many families, each unit a smaller picture of the bigger church. As we develop this healing place in our marriage, it spills into our families, and then, finally, into the family of families. This is how the church realizes the full and total healing and sanctification that is available to her – one marriage at a time, one family at a time, until the bride of Christ finally and fully looks like Jesus!

God is that gentle healer and is calling us to take on His demeanor and gently hold our spouse in the places of their deepest pain. Look how tender He is in Paul's letter. He is the Father of mercies and the God of all comfort. This is His nature when He comes to heal, and so should it be ours also.

We would be wise to realize that God has joined us to our spouse to do some really deep heart tissue healing. When you get a deep tissue massage, the masseuse will tell you to drink lots of water because your body releases lots of old toxins that have been

---

5. 2 Corinthians 1:3-7 emphasis added

trapped in your muscle tissue for years. You can even get sick and nauseous from this kind of massage.

The same has been true, in my experience, journeying into these deep wounds with my spouse. My ugly comes out, and when it does, that's when we can finally confront and deal with it. It takes a lot to get there, so God has designed this marriage relationship to be the catalyst. The deeper you go, the more freedom there is to be found. That's precisely the point Paul is making here; "As we share abundantly in Christ's sufferings, so through Christ we share abundantly in comfort too."

We all have been wounded, but once we receive healing, we become wounded healers. The comfort that we have received, we can now transfer. That is the hope of the gospel marriage. I receive my spouse as they are, and fight like hell to get them to who they are becoming.

This stuff is hard. No Bible verse makes journeying into the mess of your past easy, but this is the promise that I can make to you: ***your past does not define you.***

The enemy would have us believe that going there and opening up that Pandora's Box will give our spouse another reason to leave. He will convince us that these memories are better left behind and hidden, but the truth is that when a wound is left unhealed, it colors and permeates everything that flows out of us. Our anger, worry, control, or lack of empathy, is all symptomatic of something deep in the soul that never got dealt with.

The past does not define, but it does have the power to inform. It can tell us why we react the way we do. It can open our

Unraveling the Past

eyes to stress triggers. It can give us tools to react better to our spouse. It also informs our spouse and empowers the great weapon of empathy.

Once your spouse knows why you react the way you do, you'll see a great wave of empathy flow over your marriage and following that empathy, grace, and acceptance.
To be fully naked and without shame, and have true and biblical intimacy means going there with your spouse. When you have someone who loves you and will stick by you no matter what, then you can go deeper than you ever thought you could go. The things that have stayed hidden and festering way below the surface can finally see the light of day, and the hope of healing can begin to manifest.

If we cannot overcome it, then we can absolutely expect to pass it on to our kids. This is called the **Generational Curse**.

There are hurts that we don't do the work to find healing in, and, in avoiding them, we actually pass them to our kids. The things I am overcoming are the very things my dad failed to overcome, and his dad before him. You can actually track this back if you sit and think about it for a second. Your vices, your demons, they are the same that have plagued your family for generations.

This is because we are afraid to open ourselves up to the promise of the gospel marriage, that we can be fully naked and without shame. Instead, we hide. And when we do, the shame germinates, takes root deep in our hearts, and manifests into hurting the ones we love the most, ensuring they, one day, do the same. Then these specific curses stick to the generations of our families like the gum on the front of my Prius.

"The apple don't fall far from the tree." How perfect is this phrase? This concept goes all the way back to the fall! Adam passed on sin and death to his sons. Eve passed on worry and anxiety to her daughters. This happened because of the choices they made in real-time.

This is not merely some Bible story; this is the story of our lives. Things Adam and Eve said to their children, informed them on how they should talk to their future children. The ways they reacted to them showed them how to react to the very same things with their future children. And on and on it goes, even on until today.

My dad spoke over me the curses that have plagued me. My mom reacted to me in a way that has me faking it and performing today. We're at a fork in the road. We either dig into those hurt places and find healing in purging them from our lives, or pass them right on to our kids and repeat the cycle. *The power of the gospel marriage is that we are unraveling even the curse that was passed onto us and will try and pass its way through us to the next generation.*

THE CHILD WOUND

"Is your Father really good?" This was the first lie ever told, and we've been asking this question ever since. I know my dad did the best he could with what he had. In fact, he would often tell me that he was doing the best he could. But he is fallen. Like I am fallen. The enemy is wise to exploit this fact because if we can learn to doubt our fathers on earth, then we can surely learn to doubt the True Father in heaven. This has always been his tactic, and it works, unless a miracle takes place, so why stop now?

When our parents fail us, we find ways to navigate around the hurt that it caused us subconsciously to keep on surviving. The enemy likes to insert himself when we are very young and first learning to cope with that very real failure so that he can take advantage of our naiveté and spin his own narrative on what's happened to us, as he did with Eve, "Did God really say you couldn't eat of any tree?"

Same Enemy. Same tactic. Different day.

It has been helpful for me to understand this concept with this defining word: "**Agreements.**" The enemy wanted Eve to make *an agreement* that *maybe* God wasn't as good as He had said He was. Once Eve was willing to make that small adjustment in her thinking – the *maybe* – then the hook was set, and Satan had control of the narrative.

If our enemy can incept that idea into our minds, especially at a young age where we haven't developed the tools to correct the record, then he can build a whole false narrative from that agreement. We can come to believe certain things and act in certain ways based completely and utterly on lies, that might even be decades old, told to us when we couldn't even tell a lie from the truth.

The work to deconstruct these lies and the worldview that emerges upon them might take as long as it took to construct them! That's why God has designed marriage to be life-long. In His grace, He has given us this powerful counselor in our spouse. They are committed to stay, they've got skin in the game, and they are surrounded by the God of all comfort as they step into those wounds. Marriage is that one relationship uniquely designed to unravel these wounds because it is the covenant to love what has been declared, by time and pain, unlovable.

One evening, my mom came home very angry to a house that was supposed to be cleaned by her three children, but wasn't. She was enraged. She threw things and yelled things and the whole event is seared in my brain.

I can still recall all these decades later, the rage on her face. I can still picture the whole scene like I'm watching it from the outside. She called me and my siblings "the spawn of Satan." My dad stood idly by. I remember his passivity, and that I begged him to intervene, but he wouldn't, or maybe he couldn't. His dad never did, so why would he be any different?

So I ran. This wasn't the first time that I'd "run away," but this was the farthest I'd ever made it before realizing the chaos of home was better than the chaos of the outside. I was eight years old, after all.

I hid in the back of the family minivan. This part I suppressed, and it's come to light recently – I made *an agreement* with the enemy that night. She called me the spawn of Satan, and she was my mother, so she was the devil, and my dad was her pawn, powerless to stop her rage. The enemy didn't mind his name being used, he fed me every damn word.

Fast-forward almost thirty years, Jules sent me to the mountains of Colorado with the goal of doing some soul searching. Wise woman. I was so angry at my dad for not giving me a legacy, not teaching me what it is to be a man, and for not teaching me how to love a woman, or lead a child.

There was a moment in that frustration when I started yelling at the trees, and the phrase came to my lips, "I'm the spawn of Satan, I have no legacy." I actually said it out loud.

My eyes welled with tears.

I realized that I had made this *agreement* with the enemy, and it stole my ability to see all the good my parents had ever done. He took a moment of great weakness in my parents and let it spin into a narrative he could control. It had colored, for me, every action they did from there on out as "not good enough" and "less than what it could have been." I used this as an excuse to quit when things got tough. I used this as an excuse to accept mediocrity in my marriage and as a father. "I am like my father before me," I would believe.

Right after this moment of clarity, a flood of memories came into my mind of my dad teaching me how to change a tire and the oil in a car. I had images of him showing me how to bring life from the dirt, order into chaos. I saw that he was still with my mom through all of it. I saw my mom's strength and that she never backed down when things got hard. That I come from a line of strong people surviving the hardest things. The enemy had tried to steal all that from me. And then the wildest thing happened, my heart filled with empathy.

When I got home I began to recount to Jules all that God had brought to light, and she warmly responded, "I have been waiting for you to see this."

This began, for me, the journey of delving into the suppressed hurts that had shaped the way I think and feel. All the *agreements* I had made to hide my shame and perform so I could be accepted were starting to be exposed. Jules was there every step of the way, because the gospel marriage is absolutely designed to be the place where we unravel the deepest and most hidden parts of the curse.

It took thirty years for this lie to find the light of day, and I can honestly say that the greatest unraveling of the curse has been through my marriage with Jules.

A LINEAGE OF BLESSING

There is a trap of the enemy here that we must be careful not to ensnare ourselves in, as I had. Yes, there is brokenness passed down to us from our fathers and grandfathers. Yes, some curses have ravaged our lineage for decades upon decades. Yes, there is very real hurt that we must encounter, embrace and find wholeness through. But the enemy would have us focus only on the pain.

The enemy would have us discount the strength of our family. That day I broke the *agreement* I had with the enemy, I began to see what my family was, and stopped only focusing on what my family wasn't. I began to see my uncles bass fishing in Washington, my grandfather's reservoir of knowledge, my grandmother's wit. All of this is in me! All of this is also flowing in my veins.

When we accept the lies of the enemy about our families, then he can also cut off what blessing and strength has come through our blood. This is how he systematically dismantles the power and presence that our lineage could be. We must no longer let him!

Here's a battle strategy for you in embracing the good in your family tree and activating it in your family's future. Draw out a legacy tree. This isn't just a family tree with names and dates. Write down the strengths of the individuals.

What did your dad do well?
What strength did you see in your mom?
What are your uncles or your aunts known for?
What about your grandparents?

Write it down, track it back and see that God has been passing the wild creativity of Adam right on down to you. God has been faithful to bring through the daughters of Eve, her fierce passion.

A NEW FATHER

The great hope of the gospel is that we actually have a new Father. We have been adopted, and our souls cry, for that perfect Father has been realized by our True Father, God. That's why Paul declares,

"For all who are led by the Spirit of God are sons of God. For you did not receive the spirit of slavery to fall back into fear, but you have received the Spirit of adoption as sons, by whom we cry, 'Abba! Father!' The Spirit himself bears witness with our spirit that we are children of God, and if children, then heirs—heirs of God"[6]

Not only do we now have belonging, and not only has the eternal cry for a True Father been heard, but we are His heirs. And not just heirs of stuff and riches, but heirs of His nature. This re-

---

6. Romans 8:14-17a

alization literally changed my life. Just as I was doomed to repeat my father's mistakes, just as I was cursed to inherit my mother's woundings, I am now destined to take on my Holy Father's likeness instead. I can be like Him. I can love like Him. I can be like my Dad. His nature is available to me.

Not only is God our Father healing our past, but He is also promising a better future.

God, the Father of all comfort, has brought your spouse to you to be the threshing floor of the deepest parts of your soul. They have been selected by the Sovereign God for your shaping, healing, and wholeness.

If your marriage is in a season of hardship, then it might be wise to start asking the Father of mercies exactly what He's up to. Maybe there is more going on under the surface than you are even aware of. You can trust him. He knows what He's doing, and even what the enemy means for evil, He works out for good.

Paul writes again in his letter to the Romans that our new Father, who has adopted us, is working out all things for our good, "And we know that for those who love God all things work together for good, for those who are called according to his purpose. For those whom he foreknew he also predestined to be conformed to the image of his Son."[7]

You see what's happening here? We sometimes seem to think that God is taking bad situations and making them good, or that God is taking us out of bad situations altogether, but that's not what this text says at all.

---

7. Romans 8:28-29a

Unraveling the Past

This is the declaration that our Father is bringing us *through* the tough stuff faithfully all the way *to* the good. And then Paul goes on to define what that good is: *we are being conformed to the image of His Son.* God is allowing what's happening on the outside of our physical bodies to conform us on the inside all the way to the soul. The goal is that we look like Jesus. This is the purpose He has called us into in and through marriage: to show Christ in the fullness of His glory, and the love and adoration of the church.

One of the most beautiful realities of the gospel marriage is that God brings forth the healing promised to us all throughout the Bible by means of community. We are healed as we are exposed and accepted, and primarily in the context of conflict in relationships, "As Iron sharpens iron, one [person] sharpens another."[8] It's the steady grating on each other where God brings forth the best versions of ourselves.

These wounds might stay hidden and festering if not for the relationships arounds us. How much more the marriage relationship! The truth is, we need each other. It's only in relationships where we can experience true wholeness.

---

8. Proverbs 27:17

THE JOURNEY OF INTERDEPENDENCE

We spend twenty or thirty years learning how to be independent. In fact, this is the whole goal of growing up – learning to take care of ourselves. Then we are joined to our spouse and have to start taking care of someone else, who has been trained to take care of themselves. We then spend the next few years realizing how broken we are, and all of this can run the danger of pushing us from a place of mutual *independence* to *codependence*.

Codependency is where we start to rely on our spouse to meet every emotional and physical need. We cut God out, and they become our god. This is how Adam and Eve were after the fall – left alone with only each other, and that didn't quite turn out so well for them or their kids.

A big sign of codependency is when we become willing to stop letting the other person grow. We either put them on a pedestal, where they can seem to do no wrong, or we feel that we are so superior to them that they cannot speak into our lives.

Another common way I see this fleshing out all the time is that we can't admit that our spouse can change. If they are changing and growing, but we are not, then we might feel abandoned, so we chain them to who they used to be to mitigate the threat of them outgrowing us. Or, we refuse to see the change until they are so frustrated that they abandon the path to change. The deep need for them to be with us doesn't move, and neither does our progress in becoming the person God is shaping us to be.

The goal of the gospel marriage is *interdependence*, which I like to think about as the husband and wife's journey to oneness while running after God.

In interdependence, I rely on my spouse to push me to my greatest and real need, which is Jesus. I *need* her to remind me I really *need* Jesus, and she needs me in the same way. The gospel marriage not only creates the place for change to happen, but it *necessitates* change from the inside out and in the deepest places.

Interdependence allows our ugly to come out, be identified for what it is, and necessitates the change only God can bring. The depths of our hearts are slowly being revealed as trust grows, and then God can do the surgery on those deep wounds to bring real healing.

UNRAVELING THE CURSE

The promise of the gospel is not just to unravel the deep wounds of your past, but it also ensures a new and better future. Your wounds made whole actually make you stronger. As you heal from the traumas you've experienced you actually learn how to cut off the curse over your kids in that area.

While it's true we sometimes can overcorrect and hurt our kids by sheltering them from the ways we have been hurt, we are like a pendulum slowly swinging closer and closer to center. Each generation will get better and better until we see the fullness of healing come over the legacy of our whole family.

The scope of healing from God's perspective is vast. He isn't simply looking at one life, or one marriage, or even one family.

He is looking at generations, people groups, communities, and cities; He's looking at the church.

Oh, yeah, this is all about Christ and the church. As we do the soul work of unraveling the past, we are becoming the unblemished bride of Christ. This is how He's doing it – the same way you are doing it with each other.

The gospel marriage is making all things new, even the old tangled messes of our lives.

Unraveling the Past

Chapter

The Fruit

It's no accident that Paul writes about fathers and sons directly following the chapter on the gospel marriage in his letter to the Ephesians. The fruit of the gospel marriage and of showing Christ and the church is life. It's life for your relationship; it's life for your sex life; it's life for the church. This is all beautifully personified in your children. The fruit of your marriage is literally life. It's your kids; the curse wants to pass through you to them.

In fact, it was destined to be so, until Jesus radically stepped onto the scene, absorbed the curse on the cross, and made a way for the Father to adopt us into His Family. We now have a new destiny. No longer are we doomed to repeat the curse, and we have access to the first blessing.

Do you remember back in Genesis where it says "and God blessed them?"[1] The blessing was that *life* would come out of Adam and Eve's marriage, that life would multiply across the entire earth, and that that life would have a gospel purpose. He goes on to say, "Be fruitful and multiply and fill the earth and subdue it, and have dominion over the fish of the sea and over the birds of

---

1. Genesis 1:28a

the heavens and over every living thing that moves on the earth."[2] The mission and great adventure that was destined for Adam and Eve is now your and my mission. And it's your kid's mission. It's the supreme calling of humanity – multiply, and together with your kids, go take the ground and have dominion over it, and bring all of creation under the righteous rule of Jesus. We are called to go out into the wild frontier of our jobs and schools and return the chaos to order.

The curse stole mission from us. It separated the focus of husband and wife and made them forget that all along, they had a mission to accomplish – *together*. The enemy took dominion over the earth,[3] but the cross has returned it to its rightful Lord, Jesus, the Second Adam.

Now, together with our families, the privilege to unravel the curse and return the earth back to the righteous ruling of God's kingdom has been restored to us.[4] Now more than ever, this is the great adventure and calling of the gospel family. We have a real enemy and eternity at stake. The gospel is unraveling the curse and restoring all that has been stolen by it.

The earth has been patiently waiting with great anticipation for this restoration. Look at what Paul says, "For the creation waits with eager longing for the revealing of the sons of God. For the

---

2. Genesis 1:28b

3. It's worth noting that the Bible seems to argue that Satan took the dominion promised to the first Adam in Luke 4:5-7 and elsewhere.

4. Revelation 5:9-10, "Worthy are you to take the scroll and to open its seals, for you were slain, and by your blood you ransomed people for God from every tribe and language and people and nation, and you have made them a kingdom and priests to our God, and they shall reign on the earth."

The Fruit

creation was subjected to futility, not willingly, but because of him who subjected it, in the hope that the creation itself will be set free from its bondage to corruption and obtain the freedom of the glory of the children of God. For we know that the whole creation has been groaning together in the pains of childbirth until now."[5] Who is it that sets creation free? Our sons and daughters. The sons and daughters of God will rise up with the Spirit of God, and finally set right all that was lost at the fall.

This verse has tripped me up for years because of the phrase in the middle: "creation was subjected to futility, not willingly, but because of him who subjected it, in hope…" Who was this that subjected creation? Was this Satan? He wouldn't have hope that it would be free, so, it must be God, who subjected creation to Adam and Eve in the hope that they would keep it free! He passed this great authority to humanity.

This was always the plan; this was the design and purpose of the original family, but they forfeit it. That's what the curse does; it forfeits the true responsibility for a counterfeit. But the original hope of creation has been restored finally now through Jesus, the Son of God, who is now calling for the adopted sons and daughters of God to rise up and together free the earth!

It is our *great responsibility and privilege* to end human trafficking, care for animals, protect climates, restore endangered species, ensure racial reconciliation, develop systems for the impoverished to find wealth, and on and on until the earth is completely and totally free! Remember, this was the very first job given to Adam – serve the garden and protect it. It was too big for him alone and so God brought him Eve. And now we see that it's too grand a

---

5. Romans 8:19-22

mission for the husband and the wife alone (though the gospel marriage would get us pretty close!), so God has called us to invite our kids into this great adventure!

I want to take a second to caveat that kids are *not* a requirement.

The gospel marriage brings life wherever it goes. Also, the earth is pretty full, so the argument could be made that that part of our gospel mission is complete, and now it's time to bring the chaos into order.

How much better can the opportunity to accomplish this mission be than for the gospel married couple that don't have kids to raise? Your full focus can be thrown into that mission. The gospel also penetrates all these systems to which our culture ascribes to. In fact, Paul calls Timothy a son in the faith. He takes an intentional paternal role over Timothy and mentors him to full spiritual maturity. He even leaves Timothy as the pastor of one of the churches he had planted.

SHOWING THAT GOSPEL LOVE

The gospel marriage is the beginning of raising gospel kids. When we get it right between the husband and wife, the grace of the gospel saturates our homes. When we learn how to love our spouse as they are and allow God to develop them into who they are becoming, the effect we have on our kid's futures is undeniably great. When we love each other in a way that says, "I see your shame, and I'm not going anywhere," we actually invite our kids into that belonging and give them the security that they are loved, valued, and accepted before we even say a word. It starts in the marriage.

The reverse, unfortunately, is also true. Divorce is so hard for kids because it communicates that no relationship is safe. It makes them question, at a fundamental level, "Am I loved for who I am or how good I am?"

As we saw in chapter five, divorced couples are much more likely to have divorced kids. Why is that? Because we can't but pass on our curses and victories to our children. We harness this reality when we let our kids see us love our spouse and keep choosing to stay. We communicate to them that we will stay no matter their faults, and we teach them how to one day stay when they are in a marriage of their own.

Secondly, we have the privilege of training our children. The wisest parent who ever lived wrote, "Train up a child in the way he should go; even when he is old he will not depart from it."[6] I love the phrasing here – when he's older, he'll come back to it! It might feel like your kids are ignoring it, or worse doing the opposite, but you are setting a foundation that will be there, always under the surface, until they need it.

This is the promise to parents: be diligent to invite them into the story of the gospel, give them a taste of the love and joy and peace that comes from knowing Jesus, and when they are ready, just like you had to be ready, they won't be able to depart from it!

---

6. Solomon in Proverbs 22:6

The cart has to come before the horse on this. If you are telling your kids to love in a way that you yourself are not having victory in then they will develop a kind of cognitive dissonance that might fracture their belief system. Love your spouse, then train your children. Loving your spouse will actually give you the tools to train your children – the same tools that must be developed to learn how to be married well will equip you to parent well. Seek first the kingdom of Greatest Father and everything else will be added to you![7]

THE COMMANDMENT WITH A PROMISE

After Ephesians chapter five, the great gospel marriage chapter, Paul gives us a few short verses on children. "Children, obey your parents in the Lord, for this is right. 'Honor your father and mother' (this is the first commandment with a promise), 'that it may go well with you and that you may live long in the land.[8]'"

The phrase, "the first commandment with a promise" changed the way I think about some things. The fact that Paul quotes this from the Ten Commandments is actually pretty interesting in itself. Paul is the one, after all, who so eloquently expounded on the gospel in the book of Romans, definitively showing that we are no longer under the law of Moses, for it could not bring us life. Here, now, he is quoting it and urging it to be followed?! Not only that, but he says that following it will actually give you a long and good life.

The secret, I've found, is hidden in that phrase, "This is the first commandment with a promise." When Moses received the

---

7. Matthew 6:33

8. Ephesians 6:1-3, Colossians 3:20 is also similar

Ten Commandments, only one had the caveat of the direct effect of following that commandment, and that was big number Five.

Honoring your mother and father intrinsically guaranteed a better life for you then they lived because it ensures that we get better by honoring what was good that was passed from our parents.

Isn't that the whole idea of unraveling the curse? Aren't we all saying to ourselves, "Let's get this as close to right as we possibly can, so our kids have a better shot at having it even better than we did"? This promise is exponential in its return, too; the more honorable the father and the mother, the more honorable their marriage, and the more kids have to honor, the better it will go for them when it's their turn. The more we have lived into the promise of the gospel, the more that legacy will be ready to receive our kids.

This commandment transcends the law of Moses because it comes with a promise. It was always a shadow of the gospel and the unraveling of the curse. I believe that, in the New Covenant, every commandment that comes forth from our mouths should also carry with it a promise! How differently would we give commandments as parents if we had this mindset?

It's also worth noting that the gospel marriage brings honor to the concepts of father and mother. Paul is clearly talking about a married couple who are walking together in the calling of Christ and the church. That's why this chapter follows the gospel marriage. They are worthy of honor, and that honor ensures a legacy is passed to their children. As the marriage is lifted into a place of esteem and honor, everything gets better.

FATHERHOOD

Paul goes on to admonish, "Fathers, do not provoke your children to anger, but bring them up in the discipline and instruction of the Lord."[9] There's a great contrast here that is worth noting. The original Greek implies that fathers have the power to either nurture your child towards frustration or towards the Lord.

Fathers can either stunt the spiritual growth and maturity of their children or cultivate a heart that longs after the things of God and develops until fully matured. The "discipline and instruction of the Lord" can also be translated as "training and counsel of the Lord." This is that new instinct I've been talking about. The curse would say to us, "You must be like your father." The gospel smiles and replies, "Okay, here's a new Father," and as fathers emulate their new Father, they train their kids to emulate Jesus! The curse that was meant to bring us death, in turn, brings us life.

We see clearly here that fathers can stunt the growth of their kids by provoking them to frustration, but what exactly does that look like? The contrast of this verse reveals that it's merely the opposite of training them and counseling them with Godly wisdom. When fathers put the expectations of the world on their kids, give into the curse and go to work, or ignore the responsibility of spiritually maturing them, they frustrate the spiritual growth of their kids.

Paul uses almost the same language in his letter to the Colossians, shedding a bit more light on this text when he says, "Fathers, do not provoke your children, lest they become discour-

---

9. Ephesians 6:4, Colossians 3:21 is also similar

The Fruit

aged."[10] Again, the same word is used there to mean "provoking your kids to frustration." Provoking our kids to frustration can simply be understood to mean *slowly compelling them into the patterns of the curse.*

When we push our kids into the curse, just as we were pushed into it by our parents, we slowly take their fight and courage from their souls, because the promise of the cursed fruit is a lie. My dad, unknowingly I'm sure, pushed me into the curse by encouraging me not to be lazy and establishing a "good work ethic" in me. I'm not saying that these are bad lessons in and of themselves, but I understand that when they become the center of a child's relationship with his dad, it's the enemy trying to get in and continue controlling the narrative.

The gospel marriage is the fertile ground wherein Godly kids are nourished to proper development, and it's also the place where we teach our kids how to join the fight against the enemies of God and for the restoration that the gospel promises.

So if not a good work ethic and how to change a tire on a car, then what *do* we teach our kids and *how* do we connect with them? Teach them the world view of Jesus! Allow them into the adventure of fighting for your family, seeing the world the way Jesus does, and allowing them to learn how to help make decisions that grow the kingdom of God and impact the world around them. All else will be added unto you, my friends.

Invite them to go into the world and subdue it, bringing it back under the right rule of Jesus, freeing those trapped in human trafficking, opening the eyes of those caught in the prison of reli-

---

10. Colossians 3:21

gion, and proclaiming the love and belonging that is found in Jesus! I know this isn't the most practical "how not to raise little tyrants," but this is because I believe in my soul that we need a total brain rewiring on this and once we have it, our new instincts will kick in.

I also want to mention that there is a real lack of the passivity of Adam in this verse. The father is called to action. "Discipline" or "training" and "instruction" or "counsel" are the words that Paul used.[11] These are *action* words. These are *adventure* words. These are *do* words and *think* words.

Train your sons to see the world like Jesus. Counsel them to think as He does. Press in when they don't see something quite right. Don't outsource hard talks to mom. Step into the wild unknown of your kid's hearts, and bring order, belonging, and strength. Take them to baseball games and camping trips. Train them about competition and the wilderness. Speak to them of how Jesus stood up for the women trapped in adultery and about how Jesus called the pastors of the day "white washed tombs." Counsel them about love and sex. Transfer to them the mind of Christ.

MOTHERHOOD

Again and again, the Bible speaks of the joy of the fruit of the womb. "Behold, children are a heritage from the Lord, the fruit of the womb a reward."[12] Rejoice in the fruit of your womb, and remember that they are also the fruit of your marriage and of your life. Have such joy!

---

11. Paideia and nouthesia are the Greek words used and they give a feeling, to me at least, of transferring the mind of the Lord to your kids.

12. Proverbs 127:3

Solomon's words about mothers are important here: "Strength and dignity are her clothing, and she laughs at the time to come. She opens her mouth with wisdom, and the teaching of kindness is on her tongue. She looks well to the ways of her household and does not eat the bread of idleness. Her children rise up and call her blessed."[13] I love the picture here; she is loved, and because of that, she stands in strength and dignity. She is so full of joy that she cannot contain the laughter as it overflows from her.

There is so much joy available in your children, and the enemy tries to rewrite that narrative all too often. The curse seeks to tie your soul to your children. The pain of childbirth is so constant and ever-present that it can actually tether the mother's meaning and purpose to her child, putting a weight and expectation on the child they were never supposed to bear. Children were never supposed to fulfill our life's meaning. They are fruit for a well-lived life. They are a promise fulfilled in the gospel marriage, but true meaning comes from Jesus.

When you make your children your purpose, you try to use them to fill a void only Jesus can fill. It just doesn't work. Not only do you risk missing the fulfillment of your gospel marriage, but you risk losing the one thing that you actually need most – Jesus.

Often, this part of the curse creates a schism between the mother and child, even on through to when the child grows up. The child can start to feel like they are never enough, or they can never do enough to please mom. This not only creates tension in the relationship, but also in the marriage, often forcing dad to choose a side. This is another tactic of the enemy to divide and conquer. When we are wise to this tactic, we can work together to unravel

---

13. Proverbs 31:25-28

this part of the curse. Dad loves mom like Christ loves the church, displaying Christ to her every day that her joy might be from the overflow of the meaning and purpose she's found in Jesus and in the marriage.

Once that tether is healthy, then mothers become what they were always meant to be. Adam called the woman "Eve" because all life flowed from her. That was the design – life flowing from the woman, life for her husband, her kids, and her community. When a woman is fulfilled by Jesus, she is an unstoppable force that declares the resurrection wherever she goes! She can light up any room!

The power of the woman is truly unknowably deep. I've seen her comfort those who have lost everything, and I have seen her call out the most hidden parts of the most complex of deceptions. A mother's instinct to comfort and protect is so powerful that she could pick out a threat from a throng of people by her gut feeling alone. She is like the church, restoring all that she touches as she moves towards her Savior. She is like the Spirit of God, seeing the deep broken places and bringing healing and wholeness.

GET A VISION

One of the most fruitful things Jules and I ever did was write down a vision for our family. We see in scripture that vision is necessary for the unraveling of the curse God has set us to accomplish by the gospel. I've heard the verse, "without vision the people perish" about a thousand times, but did you know that this proverb is connected to another: "Correct your son, and he will give you rest; he will give delight to your heart. Where there is no vision the people perish"[14]?

There is no reason why vision and your family should be mutually exclusive. I define vision as knowing where you want to go and developing a strategy to get there. Know where you are taking your family. If you don't know, get with your spouse and figure it out. Pray and ask God where he is taking your family.

In Paul's letter to Ephesus – the same book where we find the gospel marriage chapter – he says, "For by grace you have been saved through faith ... For we are his workmanship, created in Christ Jesus for good works, which God prepared beforehand, that we should walk in them."[15] The gospel not only saves your marriage and unravels the curse, but it now sets your whole family to His unique purpose He has already designed for you. There is ground to take. There is chaos that needs to be set to order. Get a vision, and get to work!

How do we develop a vision for our family? Vision comes when the curse is unraveled. When the man turns his attention from work to his family, he will get a vision for where God is taking his family. As the man seeks to present his wife as washed by the water of the word, God will fill his heart with dreams for his wife and kids. As the woman has surrendered her husband's holiness to God, her heart will be filled with dreams of what he will become as God

---

14. Proverbs 29:17-18 KJV

15. Ephesians 2:8, 10 - I think it's worth noting that verse 8 in full and 9 includes, "And this is not your own doing; it is the gift of God, not a result of works, so that no one may boast." We are saved not of works, but we are saved for works. What kind of works? The same kind He expressed when he made us, for we are His workmanship. How cool is that?

does the work. As she wonders what her kids will become when they leave her covering, she will delight in the future God has for them. That's step one.

Step two is to invite your spouse into it. Begin to write down what God has brought you *through* and start to wonder with your spouse where God is bringing you *to*. You can actually see that outlined in our family's vision statement below. Once you have where you are going, then you can start to strategize about how you're going to get there.

Jules and I used "We do this by" and "We always" statements to remind us how we are going to get to where we are going. Be aware of how the enemy will derail your vision with blockades and distractions. Jules and I developed "We do not" statements to make sure we stay on track.

For your consideration, here is the vision Jules and I have written for our family. We go over this with the kids about twice a year, and have posted it up in our family room so we can reference it when needed. It is also a statement to all who enter our home that we are a family that is committed to seeing the gospel do its work. For a more in depth approach to writing a vision statement for your family, see Appendix 2.

THE VISION OF THE MORLET HOUSEHOLD

The Morlet family exists because God has brought us together through many joys and trials and has shown Himself continually faithful.

The Morlet family exists to glorify God in our home, build the kingdom in our city and worship God amidst the world.

We do this by:
Loving God with all heart, soul, mind and strength
Loving each other as a declaration of God's love towards us
Loving people as a partial fulfillment of the coming kingdom

We do not (because we are God's image bearers):
Yell at each other
Demean or disrespect each other
Lie to each other (for it forfeits the chance for grace)
Scheme against each other

We always:
Give each other the benefit of the doubt
End a disagreement in grace
Have each other's backs

THE GOSPEL FAMILY

The gospel family, when fully realized, is the most powerful force on earth. It is the building block that makes up the church. It is what Jesus was talking about when He said, "The gates of hell will not prevail against [the church]."[16]

Gates are defensive mechanisms. I need you to understand this. All of hell, and Satan with it, fears who you were designed to be. Read it again. All of hell, and Satan with it, fears who you were designed to be. That's why you have been under attack since your greatest grandparents.

When the family of families realizes what she is capable of, hell will fall back in terror. That's why the enemy has erected gates around hell, to protect what he has inside. The family is a weapon designed to storm the gates of hell and pull hopeless, curse-ridden people back to freedom. Fight for your marriage and your kids, and watch your enemy cower in fear, and you will have joy overflowing into every part of your life and legacy. But, most of all, you will see people freed.

"And these words that I command you today shall be on your heart. You shall teach them diligently to your children, and shall talk of them when you sit in your house, and when you walk by the way, and when you lie down, and when you rise. You shall bind them as a sign on your hand, and they shall be as frontlets between your eyes. You shall write them on the doorposts of your house and on your gates."[17]

---

16. Matthew 16:18

17. Deuteronomy 6:6-9

The Fruit

Chapter

Legacy

I know it's been quite a journey.

You now know you have an enemy.

You now have the vocabulary to first understand why marriage is so hard, and why it's so worth it to fight for it.

You're hopefully starting to get a vision for what your marriage was designed for and what it can mean for your and for your family's future.

I hope you're starting to see sex with your spouse as a fundamental weapon to wage physical war in the spiritual reality.

I hope you're starting to grasp the eternal purpose of your marriage, to show Christ and the church to an unbelieving world, and understand what is at stake if we fail.

But where is this all going? How can you and your spouse actually effectively have an impact? How is one marriage getting better going to actualize the love of God in a world that's so lost and hurting? I'm sure a few of you have thought, by now, that I'm suggesting some kind of utopian marriage that is so idealistic that it is impossible and completely out of reach for the normal marriage.

God understands all this. That's why He gives us the ***power of the day***. The sun goes down on our mistakes and rises again the next morning. And with its rise, newness. When we stack up enough of these good days, it turns into good years and good seasons, until finally, there is a life well-lived.

The power of a life well-lived is in the other lives that it touches. A life well-lived can turn into a family well-lived, then a community well-lived, and that's where the power of the gospel marriage is – it's in the community. It's in the church. Now, when a community well-lived stacks up into generations of communities well-lived, the church will become an unstoppable force of love and freedom.

And all of this starts with the spark of your gospel marriage. All of this starts with you bending grace to your spouse in the next conflict. It starts with you unraveling the curse and declaring that you will stay. It can all start today, and the effect has the potential to touch eternity. This becomes so innately practical that any one of us can start today and change the destiny of our family forever.

Let's go back to the design plan one more time, "Therefore a man shall leave his father and his mother and hold fast to his wife, and they shall become one flesh. And the man and his wife were both naked and were not ashamed."[1] Everything we have talked about really can be summed up in these couple of verses. When we understand this, our jobs will come into focus, our kids will come into focus, and our lives will become a legacy building garden of life for generations to come. And it's all deeply practical. Leave, Cleave, Weave, Achieve.

---

1. Genesis 2:24-25

LEAVE

There is a departure from our youth and covering of our parents that must take place. The importance of this rite of passage is fundamental – it's why we have a wedding. The wedding ceremony says to the community and to our families that the last chapter has come to a close, and a new chapter has begun. The wedding costs mom and dad some money because they are transferring you to your spouse.

The idea of the ancient dowry was transferring the bride and the responsibility of caring for her to the husband's family. We have moved from that custom to one of throwing a huge and expensive party! However, the principle remains the same – this is a rite of passage declaring to the world that you are no longer under the nurturing care of your parents, but are now under the care of your spouse.

Because of the curse of the soul tie, this *leaving* can be sabotaged and put your marriage in danger. This is why we fight about in-laws – it all comes back to this reality of the curse. If there was never a "full leave," the effects of that can germinate into something a lot bigger than you ever expected. As we discussed earlier, the goal of the marriage is an interdependence, running together hard after God. If we never truly learned independence from our parents, then we might sabotage the interdependence we need in marriage. When we don't fully leave our youth, then we might carry entanglements into our marriage that hinder us from fully joining our lives with our spouse.

This is true of every relationship. Once you're married, the dynamic of all other relationships must change – the journey to oneness demands it. The relationships that point you toward your spouse are the ones that need to remain. Relationships that mock your spouse or belittle your marriage must be divorced. This is a regurgitation of the first lie, "Is your Father really good? This is the spouse He brought you? Is marriage really a good thing?" If there has to be a divorce, then these relationships should be the first to go.

It might be helpful to discuss what ties might be holding you back from fully leaving your youth and the covering of your parents. I have seen decade-old marriages still struggling with this aspect of the curse because it is very difficult to identify and even harder to sort through. Paul says this great thing in his letter to the church at Corinth, "I am ready to come to you. And I will not be a burden, for I seek not what is yours but you. For children are not obligated to save up for their parents, but parents for their children."[2]

One way the enemy might try to sever the generational legacy that you're trying to build is to convince you your parents are your responsibility, or that they become your responsibility in old age. This is a dangerous road that needs to be walked with great wisdom and balance.

I also want to caveat that I am speaking in generalities here. Not all situations are the same, but I know that this is a tactic of the enemy from the curse of childbirth, and I see it in marriages all the time. I'm not saying that "leaving your" parents means cutting them off – *absolutely not*. "Leaving" is an initiation into a new level of relationship. You can even think of it as upgrading your relationship with your parents. You no longer need them to cover you

---

2. 2 Corinthians 12:14

spiritually, financially, or emotionally. You are now ready to care – because of all the tools you sharpened under their care – for others.

Honor doesn't stop, but headship and covering have changed.

The point of your legacy is to prepare your offspring to have more and accomplish more of the gospel mission than you were able to. The enemy will cut that off at the front of your marriage by convincing you to stay under your parents' covering. But, he is also more than happy to hit you in the middle of your marriage when your parents step into old age. He will lay the burden of their care squarely on your shoulders until that weight crushes you emotionally, fiscally, and finally, spiritually. The best I've seen this walked is when parents prepare for old age *to enjoy* their kids and grandkids more than they need them. This is part of setting your legacy up for success.[3] Plan on always fighting to leave, while all the while preparing to let your kids fully leave when their time has come. This is how we build generational wealth and wisdom.

CLEAVE

The "hold fast" phrase can be translated as *"cleave."* Cleave is an interesting word in the English dictionary; it can literally mean to *split* something or *stick* to something![4] I think, for the sake of this point, it's the perfect word!

---

3. I like to define legacy as the impact you have on your children and their children in wisdom and wealth.

4. dictionary.com defines it as 1. to adhere closely to and 2. to split or divide. The Hebrew here definitely means to cleave, as in stick together, but I thought it fun to mention the English ambiguity.

When couples can survive cleaving together, they often make it all the way. This is the great journey of becoming one flesh. There are ups and downs, and there are seasons of great closeness and seasons where you're fighting all of hell to bring that stickiness back. This word helps us understand that this thing that happens at the wedding ceremony isn't finished by the honeymoon. The journey of cleaving to your spouse is a lifelong journey. It is filled with great victories and defeats. The gospel marriage is the great voyage of finding your way back to your spouse in every season of life!

It's also the perfect word because couples who can't fully "leave" won't fully "cleave," and if you can't make it to oneness, then you won't make it any further. I have yet to see a couple, however, realize "leaving" and "cleaving" are essential to oneness and not build something lasting and really special. Cleaving is foundational to the marriage relationship.

Remember, as we saw back in chapter 3, that the word for "one"[5] here, in the phrase "and the two shall become one flesh," is the same word used in the famous Jewish prayer from Deuteronomy, the Shema. "Hear, O Israel: The Lord our God, the Lord is *one*. You shall love the Lord your God with all your heart and with all your soul and with all your might."[6] Our oneness is an expression and symbol of the Trinitarian nature of God!

Biblical oneness is yet another way that God has selected the marriage relationship to be a reflection of who He is. It is a compound unity. My wife and I are so different and yet becoming one. My identity has remained perfectly intact, but now has the *addition* of my wife's identity. Her skillset is now available to me in

---

5. 'e·ḥāḏ - a compound unity in the Hebrew, oneness.

6. Deuteronomy 6:4-5, emphasis added

raising our kids and building our home. My skillset is available to her to train, guide, and lead. We are two becoming one, positioned perfectly to build a legacy and the kingdom of God.

Know that Jesus does not despise oneness with His Father, but sees it as His greatest asset. That's why He is able to say, "I do not ask for these only, but also for those who will believe in me through their word, that they may all be one, just as you, Father, are in me, and I in you, that they also may be in us, so that the world may believe that you have sent me."[7] He understands that oneness is where the power of the gospel is the most potent. When you are fully *cleaved* to your spouse, the world has reason to believe that God has been reconciled to man because of your love one for another. This happens foundationally in the marriage relationship.

Your identity doesn't dissolve in the gospel marriage; it becomes more fully expressed. One of the ways you can make sure that your identity doesn't eclipse your spouse's is to invest in their hobbies. Hobbies can be an important outlet for creativity and discipline. Encourage your spouse to sharpen a skillset and invest in something of interest, and you may just find that it becomes another thing that pours wealth and wisdom in your legacy.

Cleaving to your spouse doesn't mean losing yourself; it means gaining another world.

We have sixty years to become united in heart and mind, running full speed after the heart of God. Our joys become the same. Our sorrows become the same. Our wounds heal alongside each other's and, slowly, we are no longer two, but one, showing

---

7. John 17:20-21

forever the unity that God will have with his people and the belonging available in Jesus.

It's like the joining of two great rivers – they are no longer two, they have become indecipherable and inseparable. You couldn't pull a cup of water from that new river that has water only from one half if you tried. And now their force has multiplied exponentially; the roar has multiplied, their life giving energy has greatly increased. Their reach has extended, and the power they now harness is unsearchable.

WEAVE

I'm sure you've heard the phrase "your better half." I heard this about seventy times a day when I was first married. I understand it's playful and is to compliment you for choosing a good spouse, but what it implies can be subtle in disarming the power of "two become one."

Your spouse does not complete you. They are not the missing puzzle piece to your life. Once you realize the identities you now have, as adopted sons and daughters of God, your spouse becomes the greatest threat to your enemy and *your greatest ally*. They are the power of you put to the exponential.

When we weave a life together, we bring together everything we have learned, every enemy we have conquered, our unique skills and callings, and our abilities to acquire wealth. The gospel marriage becomes a springboard for the next generation, launching them into higher atmospheres of godliness and success, slowly but surely, realizing the gospel mission of subduing the earth. The gospel marriage actually stores up in itself wisdom and wealth for you and your children. The longer we stay, the further our kids can go! The days, months, and years become roads for our children and our children's children to traverse further and longer than we did.

You'll find that the gospel marriage works – literally. I know we've talked a lot about the curse wrapping the man's mind around his work, and that the gospel marriage will redirect his focus back to his spouse. But what comes next? How do we build this generational wealth? Once our focus is realigned then we will be cleaved together with our spouse and find something to put our efforts towards, weaving a life of success together. Our strengths will be united. This is radical thinking, but I believe the gospel marriage recalibrates us to our most effective position. The weaving of us with our spouse actually becomes fuel for us to go out and conquer the marketplace with a mate who can keep us from getting out of balance, and unites our strengths to project us into the greatest chance of success.

This is how the gospel marriage actually gives us what we always wanted all along.

We, together, find a mission that we can sink our sweat into, and we begin to develop wealth and the skills to acquire that wealth, passing it on to our kids so that they might exponentially increase that wisdom and wealth themselves. Proverbs tells us, "A good man leaves an inheritance to his children's children, but the sinner's wealth is laid up for the righteous."[8] The "good man" is the one who looks forward to where his wealth is going in the future. The "sinner" doesn't realize that wealth is for so much more than the here and now. It's for generations to be positioned to bring heaven to earth. You can't keep it, so prepare your kids to sus-

---

8. Proverbs 13:22

tain it; that we might see heaven on earth through our kid's wealth and wisdom.

Like when single cords are braided together, the fabrics of your life weaved will provide the kind of strong foundation that the weight of generations can build upon. The greater your dream for the future of your family, the more you will need to be united with your spouse to sustain that vision in the here and now.

There is so much more than financial wealth to pass on to your children. The wisdom that is accumulated from doing marriage well will equip your kids to sustain wealth and have good relationships themselves. This creates the kind of infrastructure necessary to carry the kingdom of God. In fact, your relationships with your kids depend so much on the weaving of your relationship with your spouse. Out of that relationship flows an abundance of knowledge and relational awareness.

As you *weave*, you also are removing the bad cords and emotional hang-ups that have crept in over decades of hurt and trauma that would weaken your relationship. This means you are becoming the best version of a mother and father that you can be, just by loving your spouse and bending out the grace of God to each other. That parenthood becomes a lesson in parenthood for your children, and they are set up to be better parents to their children, and so the dynasty of your legacy will continue!

ACHIEVE

When you are faithful in doing this for thirty or forty years, you will turn around and realize that you have become the patriarch and matriarchs of your family, highly esteemed, and truly honored. Your children and grandchildren will go on to change the world and set so many people free. There will be so much chaos turned to order with your lineage's fingerprints all over it. This is the dream, and the gospel marriage promises all of it! Like the psalmist says about God, it can be said of you, "One generation shall commend your works to another, and shall declare your mighty acts."[9]

And in the end of days, God your Father will have found you good and faithful, your enemy soundly defeated, your spouse loved and accepted, and you will be naked and without shame. That is the greatest achievement of the marriage relationship as it works out through the gospel – you are naked and without shame!

Your enemy hates even the idea of your marriage, and he will try to stop your progress through this at every stage. He wants to tie you to your parents and your parents to you so that neither you nor they can move forward to the legacy God has for your family.

He wants you shameful and hidden so that there is no cleaving to your spouse. He is scheming to steal your generational wisdom and wealth by stopping the weaving of your lives together. He can't have you established and able to hold the weight of the plans God has for the life of your family. And finally, he is dead-set against you achieving the promises that have been laid before you because, if you do, then he is defeated.

You've got to back up and, again, remind yourselves what is truly at stake. When your marriage thrives and pushes through these seasons, you strengthen the church in exponential ways that

---

9. Psalm 145:4

we can't even understand. The impact of the married life lived well goes so far beyond the couple.

EMBRACE THE SEASONS

Understanding that everything in this life comes in seasons can be key in thriving through the hard times. Probably the second wisest man who ever lived wrote this:

"For everything there is a season, and a time for every matter under heaven:
a time to be born, and a time to die;
a time to plant, and a time to pluck up what is planted;
a time to kill, and a time to heal;
a time to break down, and a time to build up;
a time to weep, and a time to laugh;
a time to mourn, and a time to dance;
a time to cast away stones, and a time to gather stones together;
a time to embrace, and a time to refrain from embracing;
a time to seek, and a time to lose;
a time to keep, and a time to cast away;
a time to tear, and a time to sew;
a time to keep silence, and a time to speak;
a time to love, and a time to hate;
a time for war, and a time for peace."[10]

This could not be more true. I will often tell my wife, in the warmth of the summer season of our relationship, "Enjoy every moment and soak it all in, because baby, winter is coming." When we stock up joy in the fun seasons of marriage, we can withstand the long winter months of tragedy and the pains this life will in-

---

10. Ecclesiastes 3:1-8

evitably bring. The slow weaving of our lives, together with our spouse, necessitates that we endure these seasons, look back, and realize that the hardest seasons are the ones that brought us the closest together. That is the beauty of the gospel – the darker it gets, the brighter the light can shine through.

Recognizing the seasons will also give you the vocabulary and wisdom to make the most of that season. When you look at your spouse, and everything is good, store up that joy. Blow some money, travel, and woo afresh your spouse while soaking up the sun in that summer season.

When the hard times come, know that winter is here. Hunker down, be purposeful in drawing near to your spouse, pull out the photo albums, set intentional time aside to sift through the compost pile, rekindle the hearth of your sex life, and remind yourselves that this too will pass.

When the spring is sprung, go to work. Make some money and invest together in your financial future, but keep in mind that even these things should be our focus only seasonally.

When you feel the briskness of fall begins to inaugurate, know that some things need to start to die – some ministry seasons, some business endeavors, and some hobbies need to slow.

The wisdom to recognize the seasons and put vocabulary on them will not only help you to thrive through them but will also help you to get the most from them.

I think it's important to note that Jesus believed we are in the harvest season of all human history. Since He became man and walked among us, He has ushered in a new epic of history, and He has invited us into it. This is why the mystery of marriage: Christ and the church, has now been revealed. It's time to declare salvation and see heaven come to earth!

This is why Jesus says, "My food is to do the will of him who sent me and to accomplish his work. Do you not say, 'There are yet four months, then comes the harvest'? Look, I tell you, lift up your eyes, and see that the fields are white for harvest. Already the one who reaps is receiving wages and gathering fruit for eternal life, so that sower and reaper may rejoice together. For here the saying holds true, 'One sows and another reaps.' I sent you to reap that for which you did not labor. Others have labored, and you have entered into their labor."[11]

The time is now. The work has been finished by the law, the prophets, and now, finally, Jesus. He has chosen for us to reap that harvest. He has chosen for the family of families to finish the task given to Adam and Eve, "Be fruitful and multiply and fill the earth and subdue it."[12] The earth is to come under the rulership of heaven. It's time for this promise to be actualized, and I believe that will happen when the gospel marriage realizes its power. This is the greatest legacy we can have on this earth. This is what this has all been about.

LEGACY OF FORGIVENESS

The gospel marriage works itself out through conflict, which is inevitable along the journey of being naked and without shame. Therefore, we cannot escape pains and offenses along

---

11. John 4:34-38

12. Genesis 1:28a

the journey of marriage. Forgiveness is the only covering that can replace shame; it's the "anti-fig leaf" and is essential to the gospel marriage.

As forgiveness and repentance stack up in your marriage, so does the grace and presence of God. Forgiveness and grace are actually how God lives in and through your marriage. When you forgive, you are like God, and He is in your midst. As we are becoming one, it is grace that holds the whole thing together. This is why so many marriages fail – they are missing the essential ingredient of forgiveness. It's the glue and the knots of failures forgiven that become the strength of our marriage.

Acceptance only has meaning when it is bent out in grace. And out of the gospel marriage flows forgiveness to our kids and out to the rest of the church, inviting God into every aspect of our lives. This is when the church will realize her power to conquer hell – when forgiveness becomes our greatest weapon. The beauty of forgiveness is that it can now be given when it's undeserved. That's the definition of grace. We have freely received it, though it was undeserved. So, now we can give it, especially when it's undeserved.

LIFE AFTER KIDS

There is a notable surge in divorce after the kids have left the house. This is often because there is a tendency to sweep difficult things under the rug and avoid the soul work necessary from our childhood wounds and use the kids as an excuse to do so. We will avoid conflict for the sake of the kids, and when they are gone we're left with a mate we don't even know anymore because the curse had us silently missing each other for decades. The gospel marriage unravels this reality before it even becomes one.

We have to allow the Spirit of God to do the work of sanctification during the time the kids are in the house so that when they leave, there is a oneness un-flinched. We also, as I've stated many times over, need to teach and equip our kids to do the same with their spouses. If we are scared of the conflict and therefore refuse to go there, then we will pass the fear of the conflict on. This is why, in the reverse of the curse, the man is called to sanctify his wife. He must decline the route of passivity and engage in the word of God to see his wife holy. This process, as he fumbles through it, will have him clinging to God and the whole family will also draw nearer in that process.

One of the main reasons why the marriage union is so important is to raise good kids who are ready to have their part in the world and are equipped to make the world a better place. This mission doesn't stop after your kids are out of the house! In fact, I think that the stability of your marriage is even more important once your kids are gone. The world is a shaky foundation, especially in your early twenties, as you're entering the workforce and testing the waters of your own future marriage relationship. It's vital for kids to know that it can be done and done well, and they need a safe place to land when the world out there and the enemy kicks their teeth in.

One of the ways we can get mixed up in our identity is to believe that it's only found in being a dad or a mom. The earliest years of parenthood, especially, can take so much time and focus that you might start believing a parent is all that you are. I have met so many young men who have started to believe that a dad is all they are now.

While the father role is of absolute importance, it is not the center of who you are. Your identity has been found in Jesus. You are first a son, then a father. You are first a daughter, then a mother. Your life is more than your kids. It's the legacy of your entire family as you discover your role within the family of families.

Grand-parenting is also a beautiful way to ensure your legacy is built to last. When you are available to pass wisdom on to your grandkids and help raise them, you are freeing your children to continue building equity into the family, and you're ensuring that your children's children have an even better chance of getting it right. You are also establishing the idea of the gospel marriage into your family the longer you stay.

As we stay, our children learn the idea of staying because they see it in action every day. As you experience and share the fruit of staying, your children will begin to understand the value of staying for themselves. Imagine all the things you will pass to your children, having lived into the gospel marriage! Jesus will flow in and through your marriage onto your kids and their kids. Your kids will understand the power of the gospel through you!

THE LEGACY OF THE GOSPEL MARRIAGE

Leave. Cleave. Weave. Achieve. How amazing is the heart of God to give us this road map in the very first pages of the Bible? If we've seen anything it's that His word is powerful, speaking straight to the deepest darkness in the heart of man, all the while revealing and enacting the rescue plan to restore all that has been lost. How amazing is Jesus? The gospel marriage's greatest legacy is showing the redemption that is found in Jesus. Every year you make it, you are declaring that God and man are reconciled, and through that reconciliation, husband and wife are made one.

Legacy

Chapter

The Gospel Single

I'm not going to try to squeeze in a chapter about living out your singleness in a book about marriage. This isn't the "skip if you're married" chapter. I fundamentally believe that married couples are to disciple unmarried people and when they do, singles will thrive like never before in that context. I believe the gospel marriage not only produces godly children that need training in the ways of marriage and relationships, but that it is a building block providing stability for the whole church. I also believe that not all people are called to get married, but that all marriages in the church are called to provide solidity and the working out of the gospel for single people.

The wisdom and strength required to make the marriage work is the fundamental strength and wisdom required to make every relationship work, and that needs to be taught and practiced in real life-on-life relationships.

What would it look like for your marriage to be a beacon of hope for all the people in your sphere of influence? When you get a scope of this mission, it changes the way you think about your marriage and your family. It informs the vision of your home, and it even gives your kids a mission and a wild God-filled adventure. Your home will become a refuge.

OPEN UP YOUR HOME

Jesus said, "By [love] all people will know that you are my disciples, if you have love for one another."[1] We can often get stuck thinking that it's by some preaching or some Christian t-shirt that the world will know we follow Jesus. This either has us minimizing our calling in being His witnesses, or has our closet full of "a breadcrumb and fish" t-shirts![2] It's our love that reveals who we are! It's our ability to forgive and accept that is reminiscent of Jesus. If this is true of people who follow Jesus, how much more essentially true is this of the marriage relationship?

When you are living into the gospel marriage, doing the work to unravel the curse, and developing a vision for your family, *one of the best things you can do is to invite some people over for dinner.* Just opening the doors of your home to younger single people is a huge investment into the future and a declaration that heaven is coming to earth. This is how we do it; this is how heaven comes, one gospel relationship at a time, one person opening their eyes to the war that's raging around us, the reason for purity, and what's at stake if we fail. This is how we change the church and ensure the efficacy of her finishing her mission.

Opening up your home is opening up your life. When you open your life, you are ensuring that the things you've learned as

---

1. John 13:35

2. I'm sorry-not sorry if you don't get this joke. A simple Google search will bring you up to speed!

you've walked this life are passed on. The gospel marriage demands that our whole culture change.

Your marriage is not just good news for you and your family; it's good news for those that God has placed in the sphere of your lives. Even the mistakes you have made have been redeemed and serve as a roadmap for the people coming up, under, and around you.

When your kids start to understand that your home is a refuge for lost kids, their eyes will ignite with a passion to be a part of it. You will see them embrace brotherhood and sisterhood in a way that will even be fuel for their own blood sibling relationships.

They will learn how to belong as they watch you bend out belonging. They will bring people to you that need prayers. Their eyes will open to those in great need, and they will invite them in because they have seen that is how their parents are when someone is in need. As people come in, they will bring other ways of looking at the world, and your kids will inevitably develop the great strength of empathy. They will begin to see the world as Jesus does, and they will become even more effective and powerful ministers of the gospel than you are.

It's as simple as opening the door to your home, but *as complex as opening your soul to someone else*. The gospel marriage provides the belonging that makes your home a safe place for others to belong. The years you put into sifting in the compost pile and doing the hard and deep soul work becomes absolute fertilizer for your community.

Jesus beautifully exemplified this, even though He didn't even have a home. He invited himself over to meals – lots of meals. And He laughed and ate with people you'd least expect – the lost, the sinners, the people who knew they were broken. And He talked of heaven. He talked of mission and purpose. He lived life with them, forgave them, and showed them the fruit of the, "go and sin no more."

He loved, and it's a love forged in the years of loving and surrendering for His bride the church. He learned it the same place we do, in the daily laying down of our lives for our spouse.

DISCIPLESHIP IS A FIGHTING WORD

In our culture, the word "disciple" has lost its punch.

It's equated to Bible studies and circling up to share our feelings, but the word finds its origin in the word "disciplined." It's the perfect word to understand that we are in a war with a real enemy and that if we are to have victory, we will need some disciplined training and must be disciplined to pass what we've learned to our allies. We are disciplined to become like Jesus; therefore, we are disciples. We must be disciplined to meet with and mentor with younger men and women.

The scope of the fruit of the gospel marriage is so much bigger than raising godly kids! It's mentoring the next generation. This is why Paul writes to his protégé, Timothy, "Follow the pattern of the sound words that you have heard from me, in the faith and love that are in Christ Jesus. By the Holy Spirit who dwells within us, guard the good deposit entrusted to you."[3] Paul first lives it out,

---

3. 2 Timothy 1:13-14

The Gospel Single

then he teaches the systematic pattern of the gospel and how it affects real-life things like our marriage, then he encourages Timothy to guard it and pass it on. Part of passing it on is entrusting the person you're passing it to also continues to pass it on, and on and on it goes until heaven comes to earth. In fact, you are reading this right now because Paul passed to Timothy, who passed it on, and on all the way to me, who is passing it now to you.

There are people in your life who desperately need to see discipline. I'd bet they are coming to mind right now. With the gospel marriage as a launching pad, and in the season of which you agree, set up some coffee or beer meetings, or fishing trips, or a girls' night out and go start living life with these people. Once you have done the real soul work (or are in the process of doing it because, aren't we all?), you have something to offer. If you've started, then you're further than most. *The enemy wants you to think that you're not ready* for so long that you look back and realize you never even moved. He loves to see the sons of God stuck in self-proclaimed paralysis.

Husbands, go meet with some young men; your story matters. Tell them about the war we're engaged in. Tell them about the tactics of the enemy. Tell them stories of the agreements you made with that enemy and how God has even redeemed that. Tell them how you broke those agreements and are battling to see heaven on earth by loving your spouse and setting up your kids to do better. Invite them into the story of God.

Wives, go meet with some young women; your story matters. Show them how you have conquered control and anxiety. Tell them stories of the soul ties you've unraveled strand by strand. Tell them they can be loved for who they really are, fully accepted, naked, and unashamed. Tell them how the love of God has changed you so that you can now fully love others. Invite them into the story of God.

The gospel single, as the gospel marriage informs them, actually has a reach the gospel marriage might only dream for!

Paul says this very interesting thing in his letter to the church at Corinth,

"The unmarried man is anxious about the things of the Lord, how to please the Lord. But the married man is anxious about worldly things, how to please his wife, and his interests are divided. And the unmarried or betrothed woman is anxious about the things of the Lord, how to be holy in body and spirit. But the married woman is anxious about worldly things, how to please her husband. I say this for your own benefit, not to lay any restraint upon you, but to promote good order and to secure your undivided devotion to the Lord."[4]

This passage affirms what I have been saying for a bit now – that the married person is free in the gospel to focus on their spouse with an energy rivaling their focus on God. It also brings to light that the gospel single has the time and focus to really go all-in on the mission of the church! What would it even look like if the gospel-married couples rallied around the gospel singles and trained them to do the work of ministry?! Revival, I think.

---

4. 1 Corinthians 7:32-35

ADOPTED TO ADOPT

I've heard it said that the degeneration of society is when single parenthood becomes the norm. Because of the curse, the difficulty of marriage, and the schemes of the enemy, we are the most fatherless generation in history. There are over twenty-five million fatherless children in America today, and the effects of that are staggering. Children are four times more likely to be financially disadvantaged and twice as likely to drop out from school.[5] Fatherlessness accounts for sixty-three percent of youth suicides, ninety percent of youth runaways, seventy percent of juveniles in state-operated institutions, seventy-five percent of youths in substance abuse centers, and more. "Young men who grow up in homes without fathers are twice as likely to end up in jail as those who come from traditional two-parent families...those boys whose fathers were absent from the household had double the odds of being incarcerated -- even when other factors such as race, income, parent education and urban residence were held constant."[6]

The enemy has come to steal, kill, and destroy our marriages and our family, and you know what? He's damn good at it. He would see a whole generation of fatherless children repeat that same curse until we're all so lonely, broken, and fatherless, but God has stepped in and adopted us. He has become our Good Father, and He has also called us to adopt. I'm not just talking about legally adopting kids here, either. The church will win the war when she takes care of the fatherless. The most chaotic place on this earth that needs to be brought under the subjugation of the kingdom of

---

5. One study from 2012, "The Vital Importance of Paternal Presence in Children's Lives," shows that seven out of 10 high school dropouts are fatherless.

6. Harper C, McLanahan SS. Cited in Father Absence and Youth Incarceration. Journal of Research on Adolescence. 2004

God is the fatherless generation. I've heard it said, "Win the men, win the war," but I firmly believe it is better said, "Win the marriage, win the war"!

We do this, as a couple, with our money, our mentorship, and our time. God has blessed the gospel marriage with financial equity so we can undo this curse. He has made the marriage a hub of resources so we can effect real change. He has made the gospel marriage a hub of relational wisdom so that we can change the narrative of the fatherless sons and daughters. We are brought together with our spouses to pass on the wisdom we have accrued in staying with them!

God has taught *us* how to fight so we can teach the fatherless how to stay and not repeat the sins of their fathers. God has interwoven seasons in our marriage to go and loose some strongholds of the enemy and proclaim freedom to those doomed in generations and generations of the curse.

If you can adopt, adopt. Bring the fatherless in and call them sons and daughters. If this is tugging at your heart even as you read this, then it's a pretty good indication that it's time to start talking about this with your spouse. It is an investment in the future kingdom that will return as fruitful as having kids. This is that kind of hundred-fold fruit that Jesus was talking about in the gospels.[7] Every child you can bring under your roof has a better shot at being changed by the love of Jesus, and giving their life to see heaven come to earth.

If you can't adopt, you're not exempt from loving the fatherless. Meet them where they're at and build friendships with

---

7. Matthew 13:23 , 19:29

them so that they might have a better shot at the gospel marriage. Feed them! Talk with them! Start to invite them in to see what a marriage is. They need to see first-hand how to treat a woman and respect a man. Show them how to interact with their kids and how to be angry without sin. Bring them in, one meal at a time.

You've probably caught on now that I'm not really a fan of religion, but religion defined like James does I can get behind: "Religion that is pure and undefiled before God the Father is this: to visit orphans and widows in their affliction."[8] Yeah, that's in the Bible! If you want to live out some religion, then go and care for the fatherless.

NOT AN EASY THING

Though this is as simple as changing your mind about the impact your family could have and opening the door to some people in your sphere, I don't want to ignore the difficulties this could pose. You will be opening your home to some real brokenness.

As my family walks this, we are constantly telling our kids things like, "Just because so-and-so responds like that doesn't mean you have to" and "Do you see how so-and-so does that because of what's been done to them?". I have found it to be an opportunity to invite them into the story. I will literally ask them why they think someone has behaved the way they have. As they think critically and lovingly about the situation, their minds and hearts become like God's as they strive to see things the way He does. I'm trying to teach them how to fight for gospel love.

---

8. James 1:27

Use wisdom. There is not a background check to come to dinner at our house. We've set up our home in a way that attempts to communicate safety and love to everyone; regardless of their history, trauma or background. This means that my wife and I have a real, open, and honest flow of dialogue about what is wise and what is a danger to our family. If Jules just doesn't feel comfortable about a specific person, we pump the brakes and change the methodology of connection. Sometimes that means Jules will go meet with a woman alone or with some of her girlfriends who understand this gospel calling.

Sometimes that means I meet with a guy somewhere where my kids aren't, so there's no danger to them. We talk a lot, and we listen to each other's gut. We have the Holy Spirit, and He is after the same thing we are!

We also talk with our kids a lot. We constantly teach them about boundaries and debrief with them about how their time was when someone is over to visit. We watch them like hawks but refuse to shelter them. They know their safe people but they love all people. I want them to know how to fight, and I want them to know how to love the unlovable because I have been fully loved.

Sometimes, the brokenness is too great and the burden too heavy for my family alone to bear. Understanding this is also paramount. Having good friends who are in a different season of life and who understand the calling of the gospel marriage is important. There are even times where Jules and I know a couple that really needs help, but we are just not in a season to do so, so we connect them with our friends who are on mission with us. Once you start establishing this kind of community, then you will see freedom rise exponentially, and, finally, the church will be the church.

The Gospel Single

This is not meant to be a burden square on your shoulders. Try to find just one couple you can lock with and watch how God will grow that community of the gospel marriage. One will turn into three, three will turn into six, and six will turn into a whole family of families.

Use this book as a connecting point. Get a group of people all living out this unraveling of the curse, and we will see the fatherless cared for, the curse unraveled, the next generation disciplined, and our enemy soundly defeated.

Chapter 11

The Gospel Marriage

In a war, we don't need accountability partners; we need warriors. I will reaffirm what I said in chapter 1 – this is not merely a book about marriage; this is a call to arms.

I am looking for some good men and women to join me in the fight for marriage; too long has our enemy been left unchecked and in the wake of his schemes, too many marriages and lives have been destroyed, too many futures have been stolen, too many legacies have been cut off, too many children left fatherless. I am not okay with it, and it's time to do something about it. It's time to start fighting for our families.

Please, if this book has impacted you at all, pass it on. Let it be like sending up a flare to ask for other couples to get alongside you in this effort to fight for our marriages. Strength is in numbers, and a cord of three is not easily broken. A light shines the brightest when it comes together with another light. If we are to take ground, then we must do it together.

We've started something in our community called War Parties, which are groups getting together to go through this content. If you're interested in being a part of a War Party or even starting one then see Appendix 3. You don't have to be a theologian to open up your home and start building community! That's why I wrote the book. I wanted to hand you a mission with ground level strategy.

TO THE HUSBANDS

Love your wives. Love them hard like Christ did the church. Resist the trap of passivity and step into difficult conversations. I know it's hard. I'm right there with you because everything in this life worth having is hard. You can only bite your tongue for so long before all you've got is a mouth full of blood, so speak up.

Fight for the mind of your wife. Resist the trap of winning her once and never winning her again. Win her everyday. Guard your purity like it's the greatest weapon you hold in the fight for your marriage. Porneia is a trick and a trap. It's adultery, and it's not okay. Fight fair. Speak only words that harness the power of the promises of God over your wife. Say you're sorry when you mess it up and mean it. Keep your heart soft by confessing to your brothers and your spouse.

You're never too far gone. Start today. You won her once; you can do it again. Absorb guilt, even when you're confident you are right, and she is wrong. Remember Jesus on the cross, "Forgive them, for they know not what they do." What an act of love! Go to the cross everyday. Your dreams, your hobbies, your money, your job – nail them to the cross.

The Gospel Marriage

Seek with all your heart your wife and the kingdom of God, and whatever is left will bring you only life! Pursue your wife with the tenacity you feel welling up in you to succeed at work, and I promise you will win both! Out of that balance, you will overflow in the supernatural! Be the first to suggest date nights, sanctuary meetings, and family vision casting. Beat her to it! You know how to win this woman – go and do it!

TO THE WIVES

Submit to your husbands as a declaration that you are submitted to Jesus. Recognize and resist the enemy when he comes at you with his lies. You know his voice now, and you know his motives. If the end is destruction, then it's coming from him. Shut it down, or he will steal your family right out from under you.

Know that you are in a good company when you feel the urge to fix your husband. You can let that go. I promise it's the way to get what you always wanted. Fight the mom shame, fight the wife shame, fight shame now so your daughters and sons carry on less, if any. Through this journey you will learn trust, not in a man, but in Jesus. Out of you will flow life evermore. Life over your kids. Life over your marriage. Life over your friendships.

It's never too late. The power of the gospel shines the brightest in the darkest night. Fight for your marriage. Fight to see the good. Fight to see God in it all. Don't forget that God has brought you this man to make you look more like Jesus. There's always more to the story. There's always more to be uncovered when the fingerprints of God are on something. Let no man separate you from what God has joined together and called good.

TO THE MARRIAGE

We believe in you, Jules and I. With every fiber in our beings, we know that we are not unique or favored or elite. If God can shift the trajectory of our marriage, He can do it for you. You can do this.

God has brought you together because He knows that you have what it takes! Bend the grace and love of God out to each other, endure those hard seasons, and I promise, fruit is coming! Your love is a light in the darkness, a city of refuge on a hill, and an expression of Jesus, the absolute hope of the world. What God has in store for your marriage and for your legacy can't be captured in a book. It's the realization of a dynasty. Start today and watch the spark of your marriage change the world!

IT ALL STARTED IN A GARDEN, IT ALL ENDS IN A GARDEN

Man fell in the garden. The marriage was doomed to the curse in the garden. All this mess started in a garden. But look what John writes in Revelation,

"Then the angel showed me the river of the water of life, bright as crystal, flowing from the throne of God and of the Lamb through the middle of the street of the city; also, on either side of the river, the tree of life with its twelve kinds of fruit, yielding its fruit each month. The leaves of the tree were for the healing of the nations. No longer will there be anything accursed, but the throne of God and of the Lamb will be in it, and His servants will worship Him. They will see His face, and His name will be on their foreheads. And night will be no more. They will need no light of lamp or sun, for the Lord God will be their light, and they will reign forever and ever."[1]

It may have all started in a garden, but this story ends in a garden too. There is a new garden coming, with that same tree of life, and this time the redeemed will eat of it, and the war for the human soul will have been won. There will be no more accursed.

The curse will be finished, and all that will be left is the promise! The nations will be healed, and we will eat until we are full and thriving. This is the promise of our God. We will see Him fully and wonder in His presence. His name will be on our foreheads because we are those that belong, and *that belonging is irrevocable*. We are the ones who are naked and without shame. We are the ones that ended the curse that tried to steal our legacy.

That river, the one mentioned at the beginning of this section, is the gospel marriage. *Where it goes, life follows.* It is bright as crystal, honored among the generations, for out of it comes the life of the gospel and the completion of the promises of God!

Look what the prophet Ezekiel says,

"And on the banks, on both sides of the river, there will grow all kinds of trees for food. Their leaves will not wither, nor their fruit fail, but they will bear fresh fruit every month, because the water for them flows from the sanctuary. Their fruit will be for food, and their leaves for healing."[2]

---

1. Revelation 22:1-5
2. Ezekiel 47:12

Life flows from the sanctuary of the gospel work that Jesus is doing in and through our marriages. Guard what was given to you that you might see your river teeming with life, and everywhere you go, *life will follow.*

"Surely goodness and mercy will follow all the days of my life."[3]

---

3. Psalm 23

Appendix

Appendix 1 - Sanctuary

WHAT IS SANCTUARY

Sanctuary is one of those battle strategies that really helped get Jules and I into an offensive stature when it comes to the wounds and hurts that we are not only unpacking from childhood, but even from wounds that we accumulate through the marriage. I wanted to go more in depth, here, on how to do it. My prayer is that this intentional time each week would set you up to learn the skills of communication and conflict that are necessary to defeat our enemy and set up our legacies for a future of wealth and wisdom.

SET A TIME

The first step is deciding it's time to implement something like sanctuary. Again, if you are experiencing conflict on date night, side comments at bed time, and are feeling that slow drift begin to take place, then it might be time.

Gently nudge your spouse, "I heard about this thing called Sanctuary. It's us taking an intentional time each week to talk about real things that we're going through. What do you think?" Once you have explained it, tiptoed into it, or straight pulled the bait and switch (wise as a serpent, harmless as a dove) the next step is finding an hour for that very first one.

The first one is gonna be one of the hardest, so you need a place that is quiet and free of distraction. (Read it again)

You also might need a place with natural breaks in the awkward silence that might ensue. I recommend a nice restaurant that doesn't serve alcohol (won't help to numb here). The cadence of the server visiting for drink orders, then food, might be the natural cycle that helps move the conversation along.

HOW TO START

Sanctuary starts before you get there. You've collected offenses from your spouse over the past week. Some of those offenses have illuminated past hurts and opened old wounds. Here's the thing about Sanctuary. You have got to be willing to leave them better than they were when you bring them up at Sanctuary.

The concept of Sanctuary only works if your heart is ready to heal and move forward. This means that while you are biting your tongue throughout the week looking forward to Sanctuary, you need to be allowing the Holy Spirit to work in and through those wounds. Let Him gently do what He does and begin the healing process.

Pray through them. Journal about them (Hey, I don't journal, but I admire those who have found that outlet). Talk through them with the safe people you and your spouse have picked. There's this lie that when something offends us we have to voice it. This just isn't true. What I have found is that most of the things that offend us won't even make it to sanctuary because they just really aren't that important.

Appendix 1 - Sanctuary

There are some offenses that need to be voiced but you're not ready to bring them out without anger and some really nasty stuff coming out. This is also okay, as long as you are processing them with God and with those safe people in your life. The goal here is to make sure that bitterness is not starting to take root. Bitterness is one of the greatest weapons of the enemy to disarm the marriage from the inside out.

When you voice it at Sanctuary it needs to have gone through the process with Jesus of rooting out the bitterness and the Holy Spirit's work of preparing the wound for healing. If you do the work, you will see the fruit.

Okay, you found a place, you've picked a time, you've sat at the table, the water has been served, and now the awkward silence is settling in. Now what?

I usually start the process by asking one simple question: "What's on your list?" I've done the soul work on my stuff, I've prepared my heart to receive what my spouse might say, and so I am ready to hear what she's got. Defensiveness has no place here. She's not talking to hurt me, and even if she is (because she's broken just like I am) that's no excuse for me not to absorb that in this moment and make sure that this stays a safe place to bring offenses. Sometimes this is going to turn into a fight. **That's okay.** Fight fair. Volley back and forth and try to move towards resolution. Even if you make it a step further than you were, then it is so worth it.

HOW TO END

Pay the bill and leave. The bill to me is my favorite part of sanctuary. It's such a good reminder that what happened here has finality and purpose. I don't take the bill with me when I leave. It doesn't cling to me any longer. The debt is no longer owed or necessary. It has been paid in full and I intentionally leave it behind.

It's the same with the work we just did. Those things said and felt had their place and they don't need to come with me. The debt has been paid in full and I can freely leave it behind. Set it down. No matter how heavy or hard that hour was, you can set it down. And if that is just too hard, guess what? You have another sanctuary coming next week where you can pick that crap up and sift through it again.

This intentional hour doesn't work if it just keeps coming up in every crevice of your life throughout the week. I understand that this is a discipline that has to be learned and a skill to be sharpened. Work together by gently reminding each other. I use the language, "Can this wait for sanctuary?" In that moment, I'm not downplaying it, or discarding it—I am communicating that this thing is so important that I want to put it in its right place where I am ready and fixed on working on it.

Kiss your spouse. Grab their hand and walk out. You did the work, it was hard, and for that I admire your courage, and you should admire it in each other.

THE AFTERMATH

There are going to be those Sanctuaries where you walk away with a sense of wonder and awe at the fruit God has brought to your marriage. Relish those and enjoy those seasons, but remember, winter is coming. Life comes in seasons and so does your marriage. You are going to have Sanctuaries that are pure conflict;

a big ol' fight with hushed yelling while the waitress fills your water glass. This is okay. Remember the words of Paul, "Be angry, but sin not."

The key here is that when the bill is paid, the fight is over. Put it on hold and sift through it back in the secret place of your heart. Find your safe people and wrestle through the argument with a heart that is ready to hear where you might be in error. If you're doing this right, then by the time the next sanctuary comes around I'd be willing to bet that you are filled with excitement and anticipation at what God might do to move the needle even more in that conflict. If you can develop and keep this heart stature, Sanctuary will become a fountain of blessing and a well-fortified defense for your marriage.

CHOOSING SAFE PEOPLE

Once a few Sanctuaries stack up it might be time to approach the conversation about your "safe people."

Safe people are the people that you can trust to point you back to your spouse when you're in conflict. These are people, and this is key, *that your spouse also trusts to hear the dirty laundry and commit to being part of the solution.*

My wife has a best friend, Christina, who I trust implicitly to help Jules healthy vent, but who I know will point her back to me and help us build the legacy that we are committed to building. I know that when Jules goes to Christina our marriage can only get stronger. This is a safe person.

I think it's paramount that these are people that you've both agreed upon, so that your marriage would be safeguarded on all sides. Your spouse will recognize "friends" who will only regurgitate your own view back to you, or even worse, support your confirmation biases and actually make things worse. You need good friends, who like Solomon says, are willing to wound with the truth, so that your marriage might be healed: "Faithful are the wounds of a friend, but deceitful are the kisses of an enemy.[1]"

You also want friends who are rich in wisdom. Jesus says this amazing statement, "when the blind lead the blind, both fall into a pit![2]" Gathering to yourself wiser and older safe people will ensure the success of your marriage. When looking for your safe people, find people that are doing this well, not just those who are closest to you. Jules and I both have a few older safe couples that we can vent to, as well as safe peers we can vent to, for in the mouth of many counselors is wisdom.[3]

---

1. Proverbs 27:6 KJV
2. Matthew 15:4 ESV
3. Proverbs 11:14, 15:22 ESV

Appendix 1 - Sanctuary

THIS IS A BATTLE STRATEGY

Remember, this is a battle strategy. *It's not weakness to need outlets to vent.* It's not weakness to need an intentional time to channel conflict. It's wisdom. It is being aware of the enemy's tactics, and beating him at his own game. He means for conflict to be the place where your relationship disintegrates, but Jesus would see it become the place that solidifies your love and devotion to each other, and pushes you to become naked and without shame!

Appendix 2 - Your Family Vision Statement

A family vision statement will serve to be your guide when you're not sure what the next step for your family is. I developed ours in the pre-sunlit hours of the morning when the house was quiet and the kid (only one back then) was asleep. First I talked with Jules extensively about where we were at and what the mission of our family was. After writing a draft, I then showed it to Jules and she helped get it across the finish line. We have edited it here and there over the years, but the bones of it have stayed the same.

I'm not sure if this kind of method will work for your family, but if you don't know where to start, why not give this a try?

Appendix 2 - Your Family Vision Statement

THE VISION OF THE MORLET HOUSEHOLD

The Morlet family exists because God has brought us together through many joys and trials and has shown Himself continually faithful.

The Morlet family exists to glorify God in our home, build the kingdom in our city and worship God amidst the world.

We do this by:

Loving God with all heart, soul, mind and strength
Loving each other as a declaration of God's love towards us
Loving people as a partial fulfillment of the coming kingdom

We do not (because we are God's image bearers):

Yell at each other
Demean or disrespect each other
Lie to each other (for it forfeits the chance for grace)
Scheme against each other

We always:

Give each other the benefit of the doubt
End a disagreement in grace
Have each others backs

WRAP IT IN BIBLE

We mapped our statement around Deuteronomy 6:1-9. This is a passage that has resonated with me deeply since I first studied it in school. The whole idea behind this moment in scripture is legacy. It's rooted in the idea that we pass on what we've seen and heard about our God to our children to ensure that we are established on who He is. I recommend checking it out if you're struggling to find one that really resonates with you. If you do have a verse that really means something to you and your spouse then start there! This is not necessary. God has given you a vision for your family (or He is about to) and that's a good enough starting point as any.

YOUR VISION

Once you've found a theme verse, you're ready to ask a few questions about who you are and where you're going. These answers will help shape the big statement you want to make at the top of your vision.

- What has God brought us through?
- What are some key promises God has made to us as a family?
- What kind of influence do we hope to have in our community?
- What does our marriage thriving look like when we are old?

Out of these answers, it's time to write your big idea. This should start with a statement like, "The _____ family exists to..." Our statement starts with, "The Morlet family exists because..." We chose this route because we wanted to begin with

Appendix 2 - Your Family Vision Statement

how God has been faithful to us and has brought us this far. As you probably know by now, we have survived a bit, and highlighting God's faithfulness was important to ground our journey. We exist still because of God's faithfulness.

Our second statement is our big idea. You'll notice we've included a couple of sub-ideas: glorify, build, and worship. For our family, we want God to get the glory first, in and through everything that we do. We understand that starts in our home. Secondly, the Morlet family is a family of builders; we start new ministries, businesses, and our creators. This aspect of building is not for the purpose of gaining wealth or platform, however, it is for the building of God's kingdom. Worship is how we finish everything. Even the hard winter seasons are surrounded in worship. We are worship leaders and will be intentional about training our kids to be worshippers themselves. These three ideas make up the whole.

We also included the scope in which we hope to have an impact. This is intentionally: starting with the home, impacting the city, and finally, being seen in the world. We understand that we can't reach the world if our home isn't right. We also understand that we are not even worthy of being noticed in the world if we don't care about the city God has set us in. This progression of scope is intentional. You'll notice our vision is big. A vision should be something to strive for and something that takes hard intentional work to achieve. Where, in your wildest dreams, might God take your family? Spend some time with Jesus asking these huge questions. When you start to get a feel for what He might be up to through you and your spouse, write it down! Try and get it into one concise sentence. This sentence will help guide you when you find yourselves at a fork in the road or when in the compost pile real deep. If you know where you're going you are certainly more likely to get there!

HOW DO WE GET THERE?

A strong vision is not just about knowing where you're going, but also developing an idea of how you'll get there. We decided to quantify this in the "We do this by" statements. You'll notice that this is where we really connected with the Deuteronomy passage. How do we plan on glorifying, building, and worshipping? By loving. We chose love as the central "work" of fulfilling our vision statement. When you are writing your statement what "action" words come to mind. They might be love or build or cultivate. When you read your statement what does it make you feel like doing? Start with that.

Again, I thought through the progression of scope. The vision is so much bigger than we are now, so how are we going to slowly get there? Well, it starts in my domain. My domain is my heart. We are going to get there by loving God first and loving Him fully as I can. Next, I know that we will get there by loving each other. That love, though, needs to mirror divine love, which is why I added, "as a declaration of God's love toward us." There's so much gospel in that statement. He loves us, and we bend that same love towards each other. If we start there, we are sure to eventually impact the community around our home. How do we get bigger than that? Oh, yeah! We need to love those who are outside of our home!

Choose an action word and then build into these "We do this by" promises and the scope with which you want to accomplish that. Start small with something you know you can do and by promise three you'll be swinging for the fences.

Appendix 2 - Your Family Vision Statement

WATCH OUT FOR THE ENEMY

I decided to include a whole section dealing with those things that might hinder us from accomplishing our mission. We have a real enemy and he would hate to see us accomplish this mission. I know for my family there are areas where he knows we are weak, and so I commit with my spouse and kids to thwart his plans before he can even think of them. These are those spots where he might use your child wounds to keep inflicting wounding. For me, I knew our house could not be a house where there is yelling. This is not to say that yelling is wrong. If it were God would have put a limiter on our voices! My home is just not going to be okay with that kind of response. I included lying because I know that for me this is instinct. I will lie without even realizing it to cover shame, so I decided to commit to modeling truthful authenticity in my family.

I put a few line items in here for my kids too. I have a vision for the kinds of relationships I hope they have with each other. I'm not going to totally leave that up to chance though. I know the enemy and his tactics and I intend to equip my kids to stand tall against those schemes.

Even as you read this, you know the places where you are exposed to the enemy's tactics. You know the places of your spouse's wounding. Equip yourselves to defend against these in this section.

WHAT CAN YOU CONTROL?

We decided to end our Vision statement with "We always" statements. These are things that we can commit to and control. These aren't just actions, but actions that produce a culture. These are things we can remind each other of in the heat of emotion. "Remember, we promised to give each other the benefit of the doubt." "Remember, we said we'd have each others backs." I intentionally wrote this in a vernacular that was accessible to my kids. I can't make them love each other, but dammit, I can make them end a disagreement with a hug :)

What promises can you make to each other about the ways you're going to conflict? Use this section to write those down in easy and accessible promises you can remind each other.

IF IT AIN'T BROKE, DON'T FIX IT

We revisit our statement about quarterly and make sure that the kids remember it (besides the fact that we have it framed up in our entryway) and to make sure it all still applies. We make small changes to it here and there. I think twice since we wrote it in about ten years.

Appendix 2 - Your Family Vision Statement

Here, for your consideration, is a template you can use as you begin to write yours:

The Vision of the _____ Household

The _____ family exists to
_____
_____
_____
_____
_____

We Do This By:
1. _____
2. _____
3. _____

We Never:
1. _____
2. _____
3. _____

We Always:
1. _____
2. _____
3. _____

Appendix 3 - War Parties

So, the book helped your marriage, maybe even saved it, and you know in your knower that there are couples in your sphere that could really really use this. Why not start a war party?

War parties are small groups intended to spend seven weeks going through the book's content and discussing how it affects the marriages in your group.

All you need is the book, a nice open living room, and maybe the study guide (www.wedintowar.com/studyguide) if you really want to go deep. Here, in this appendix, I will go through how I recommend going through the content and how to make this thing as impactful as possible. Also, if you'd like to open your War Party to people who may be interested in your area, you can register it on the Wed Into War website at www.wedintowar.com/warparty.

BEFORE YOU BEGIN

Pray and ask that God would bring some childcare options for the group. When we go through the content I always say that children are welcome if needed because I know that couples that need it the most usually don't quite have the means or support for childcare, so we will make due with the littles around. That being said, I know that when kids are present parents can't be fully present. Pray that God would open the door for a few caretakers to come hang in a spare room or the backyard with the kiddos. Then, throw out a few feelers to some of the single people you know!

Appendix 3 - War Parties

You're gonna need some coffee and snacks! It really does make the news that we are all wed into war and have a fierce enemy who wants to kill us and destroy our marriage go down a lot easier. I usually have a co-couple that helps facilitate that. Next, as your first party is approaching, get an email list together. This will help with scheduling and will be the spot you send out questions and content to the other couples. If you're leading the group and the discussions, I recommend having that co-couple send those out diligently every session after the meeting. I also recommend recording your discussion. It is inevitable that couples will have to miss. Help them not miss a beat. All you need is an iPhone.

The setting is important. I like to have a chill playlist going to really set a calming atmosphere. Have your co-couple come a little early and set up food and get the coffee getting the room smelling great. I recommend Menga coffee for fresh aroma, and everyone knows when the coffee is good everything is good :) You can get that at www.mengacoffee.com. Use real glass coffee mugs if you got them. The details being great will subconsciously ready the hearts of your guests to hear from God. Seat chairs intentionally in pairs; nothing too obvious, but close. People will be coming who are on the brink of divorce so let's position them physically for what God is about to do in the spiritual. Pray!

One tactic I use to get couples to the study who I know really need it, but are likely going to decline, is to ask them for help making it happen. Ask them to contribute their strengths to helping these other marriages that really need it. I'll ask a great designer to come help set the mood or a wine connoisseur to pick the wine for a nightly gathering. When they feel needed they are more likely to make it happen.

WED INTO WAR IN 7 WEEKS

Feel free to send out the content schedule to your email list ahead of time. That will help busy couples determine which ones they can miss if they have to miss. Usually our sessions go about two hours, but read the room and be willing to slow it down or speed it up if needed.

The Holy Spirit really likes to mess up our plans! Also, it's worth noting that we will have couples who go through it about three times! These are usually the couples who have been starving for the community and who might have the desire to one day lead their own group. Once you have a couple show up two times, invite them to come again, but with the perspective of what it would look like to lead their own war party. Together, we can save and equip marriages and bring heaven to earth!

Week 1 - The Curse (Chapter 1 and 2)

Week 2 - Unraveling the Curse (Chapter 3)

Week 3 - Fighting Fair (Chapter 4)

Week 4 - Divorce and Porn (Chapter 5) We break up the couples at the last half hour guys and girls and talk about our secrets that we've been keeping.

Week 5 - Sex (Chapter 6) We break the couples up again to talk about our sex lives and the areas we think God might be trying to breakthrough.

Appendix 3 - War Parties

Week 6 - Leave - Cleave - Weave - Achieve (Chapter 8-9)

Week 7 - What now? (Chapter 10-11) At the end of this session we have the couples grab hands and look at their spouse and I usually say a prayer over them and end with a blessing that their marriages would be safeguarded from the enemy for legacy and bringing heaven to earth. If you are struggling with what to say for this prayer, why not use the last page of the book to read over the marriages in your war party:

TO THE HUSBANDS

Love your wives. Love them hard like Christ did the church. Resist the trap of passivity and step into difficult conversations. I know it's hard. I'm right there with you because everything in this life worth having is hard. You can only bite your tongue for so long before all you've got is a mouth full of blood, so speak up. Fight for the mind of your wife. Resist the trap of winning her once and never winning her again. Win her everyday. Guard your purity like it's the greatest weapon you hold in the fight for your marriage. Porneia is a trick and a trap. It's adultery, and it's not okay. Fight fair. Speak only words that harness the power of the promises of God over your wife. Say you're sorry when you mess it up and mean it. Keep your heart soft by confessing to your brothers and your spouse.

You're never too far gone. Start today. You won her once; you can do it again. Absorb guilt, even when you're confident you are right, and she is wrong. Remember Jesus on the cross, "Forgive them, for they know not what they do." What an act of love! Go to the cross everyday. Your dreams, your hobbies, your money, your job – nail them to the cross. Seek with all your heart your wife and the kingdom of God, and whatever is left will bring you only life! Pursue your wife with the tenacity you feel welling up in you to succeed at work, and I promise you will win both! Out of that balance, you will overflow in the supernatural! Be the first to suggest date nights, sanctuary meetings, and family vision casting. Beat her to it! You know how to win this woman – go and do it!

TO THE WIVES

Submit to your husbands as a declaration that you are submitted to Jesus. Resist the enemy when he comes at you with his lies. You know his voice now, and you know his motives. If the end is destruction, then it's coming from him. Shut it down, or he will steal your family right out from under you. Know that you are in a good company when you feel the urge to fix your husband. You can let that go. I promise it's the way to get what you always wanted. Though this journey you will learn trust, not in a man, but in Jesus. Out of you will flow life evermore. Life over your kids. Life over your marriage. Life over your friendships.

It's never too late. The power of the gospel shines the brightest in the darkest night. Fight for your marriage. Fight to see the good. Fight to see God in it all. Don't forget that God has brought you this man to make you look more like Jesus. There's always more to the story. There's always more to be uncovered when the fingerprints of God are on something. Let no man separate you from what God has joined together and called good.

Appendix 3 - War Parties

TO THE MARRIAGE

You can do this! God has brought you together because He knows that you have what it takes! Bend the grace and love of God out to each other, endure those hard seasons, and I promise, fruit is coming! Your love is a light in the darkness, a city of refuge on a hill, and an expression of Jesus, the absolute hope of the world! What God has in store for your marriage and for your legacy can't be captured in a book! It's the realization of a dynasty! Start today and watch the spark of your marriage change the world!

About the Author

Tyson Morlet is first a husband and father. He is the Creative Pastor at Shoreline Church in Austin, Texas and leads a staff of 20 and a volunteer team of over two hundred. He lives to tell and retell the amazing stories of Jesus through music, lights, color, video, the spoken word, and paint. He loves throwing himself fully into new things, whether that be brewing a beer, planting a church, or writing a book! He is committed to following Jesus radically and challenging everyone around him to do the same.